# CHAPTERS IN CHURCH HISTORY

# THE CHURCH'S TEACHING

*VOLUME TWO*
REVISED EDITION

# *Chapters in*
# *Church History*

## POWEL MILLS DAWLEY

*With the assistance of the Authors' Committee
of the Department of Christian Education of
The Protestant Episcopal Church*

**A CROSSROAD BOOK**
**THE SEABURY PRESS · NEW YORK**

COPYRIGHT 1950; AND © 1961 BY THE SEABURY PRESS, INCORPORATED
© 1963 BY THE SEABURY PRESS, INCORPORATED

*Revised Edition June 1963*

*Ninth Printing*

ISBN: 0-8164-2004-1

LIBRARY OF CONGRESS CATALOG NUMBER: 63-16290

PRINTED IN THE UNITED STATES OF AMERICA
BY THE COLONIAL PRESS INC., CLINTON, MASS.

# *Foreword*

THIS is the second volume in THE CHURCH'S TEACHING series. It takes up the story where *The Holy Scriptures* ended, and traces in broad strokes the major movements in the history of the Church down to its new ecumenical concern. It makes no attempt to be a detailed history book as its name *Chapters in Church History* implies. Such books are already available and, for the most part, remain unread by lay people. This series is not written for clergy and scholars. It is written for the average intelligent, educated layman. It goes without saying that it is not a Church School text, although parents and teachers will find it a valuable resource.

If the reader has not already read volume one, *The Holy Scriptures,* we strongly urge him to do so before beginning this book. No attempt is made to retrace that ground or to cover subjects which will appear in later books on Faith and Worship.

Here is the story of Anglicanism and our own tradition set over against the broad sweep of Christian history. It will help the reader to see the Body of Christ more clearly.

JOHN HEUSS
VESPER O. WARD

# *Preface to the Revised Edition*

THIS revision has been undertaken to correct and amplify some points at which the text of the first edition, published more than twelve years ago, has been rendered inadequate, particularly in sections dealing with aspects of recent Church history. Furthermore, the bibliography of books for reference and further reading has been completely revised, incorporating a large selection of excellent books that have appeared in the last decade. Except in a few instances, little change has been made in the main body of the text.

POWEL MILLS DAWLEY

# Preface to the First Edition

THE immediate challenge presented to the Church in each generation is to bring the redemptive power of the Christian Gospel into the historical situations in which men live. The ultimate task of the Church is to effect that redemption in terms of men's highest membership, their common life in Jesus Christ. For the Christian, this task is illuminated by the record of man's life through the ages. He finds a meaningful pattern in history, its lines etched in the everlasting vitality of the community of God's people. Church history, then, is the story of God's redemptive activity among men through a fellowship that is no less than the Body of the Living Christ. The experience of the Church in any generation transcends time to speak to men in all generations.

The task of the Church historian is not that of recording every event in the history of Christianity. Rather it is to describe those events and movements that are of permanent significance, endeavoring to indicate their meaning. An important historical discipline, therefore, is that of selection. Readers will find some familiar episodes of history omitted from these chapters.[1] If this volume is to

---

[1] The Books for reference, pages 259-268, cover in detailed fashion the various periods in the history of the Church.

fulfill its purpose, our chief concern will be to explore the meaning of important events and movements of thought, suggesting their relevance to the task that confronts the Christian community today.

While this book, like the first volume of the series, *The Holy Scriptures,* has a single author, yet in its published form it represents the work of many hands. The chapters have been scrutinized and discussed at length by the members of the Authors' Committee, as well as submitted for criticism and suggestions to faculty members of some of our seminaries and interested parish clergy. We are deeply grateful for the time and effort that many have expended to assist in this work.

POWEL MILLS DAWLEY

# Contents

# CHAPTERS IN CHURCH HISTORY

# The Church and the Roman World

G<small>O</small> YE *therefore, and teach all nations, baptizing them in the name of the Father, and of the Son, and of the Holy Ghost: Teaching them to observe all things whatsoever I have commanded you: and lo, I am with you alway, even unto the end of the world.*

The first chapter in Church history begins with the divine commission of the Lord to His disciples that closes *St. Matthew's Gospel.* As the New Testament age comes to an end, the story moves out from the early years of the Christian Church, as told in the *Acts of the Apostles,* into the wider scene of the ancient Roman world. With the beginning of the second century it has been carried beyond the historical records of the New Testament.[1]

Already the New Testament has witnessed the mighty

---

[1] The life and activity of the New Testament Church have already been described in the volume in this series entitled *The Holy Scriptures—A Survey* (New York: Seabury Press, 1961). Here we begin where that volume ends, with the impact of Christianity upon the Roman world.

acts of God that brought the New Israel of the Christian Church into being among the disciples of Jesus. Already the Fellowship has been aroused by its divine commission to bring the redeeming power of Christ into the lives of all men. Conscious of its worldwide mission, Christianity has broken out of the narrow confines of Old Israel. The Gentile mission has gone forth, empowered by the passionate conviction, as St. Paul expressed it, that *there is neither Jew nor Greek, there is neither bond nor free, there is neither male or female: for ye are all one in Christ Jesus.* Already we have had our first glimpse into the life of the early Christian communities. We have seen the extraordinary power of the Holy Spirit at work in their fellowship. We turn now to the events of the next two centuries in the life of the Church.

Before us is the record of the expansion of the Church, its early organization and development, its discovery in the terms of Christian theology of what the mighty acts of God in Christ mean to mankind. Here, too, is the heroic story of the struggle between the Church and the Roman Empire, and the ultimate triumph of Christianity in the ancient world.

### THE FULNESS OF TIME

IN A FAMOUS passage in the *Epistle to the Galatians* St. Paul used an unforgettable phrase to describe the moment in history when the Christian revelation was given to men: *When the fulness of the time was come, God sent forth His Son.* . . . St. Paul is asserting that God acted to redeem His creation when the world was ready. Christ came in a *fulness of time.*

Christians have always believed that in addition to the preparation that God wrought in the history and religion of Israel, there was a unique readiness for the Gospel in the ancient world itself. The Gentile mission met with amazing success. All over the Mediterranean basin, St. Paul and the other Christian missionaries found a ready response to the Gospel of Jesus Christ. Little communities of Christians sprang up in the chief cities of the empire—Antioch, Alexandria, Ephesus, Rome, Carthage —and in hundreds of smaller towns. Each one became a center of evangelistic activity for the surrounding area.

This triumph of Christianity was due in the end to the missionary outreach of those who knew the presence of Christ in their fellowship, and to the moral splendor of their lives. But the spiritual strength of Christianity poured into a world which was uniquely ready, even hungry for a Gospel of redemption. First-century life was spiritually restless. Religious, cultural, and political conditions in the Roman world all pointed toward a divine over-ruling of history to serve the purposes of God in the proclamation of His Gospel.

## THE ROMAN POLITICAL WORLD

As ST. PAUL and St. Barnabas sailed from Cyprus on their first missionary journey, the political power of imperial Rome was entering its final phase.[2] The circle of Mediterranean lands had long been under Roman rule. Only a few years before the death of Christ the final thrust of

---

[2] A record of the details of the missionary journeys of St. Paul and his companions will be found in *The Holy Scriptures,* ch. ix.

Roman power to the north and to the east had begun. Now as the apostles set out, the conquest is nearly complete. Roman soldiers are subduing Britain in the northwest; Roman governors are extending their authority in Syria and the other states in the east.

From the Scottish border, down the Rhine-Danube line, out to the banks of the Euphrates, the fortresses of the legions keep watch over the peace and security of Caesar's dominions. Beyond these outposts lie the trackless forests and wild steppes of central and eastern Europe, the country of the savage Germanic and Slavic tribes. As yet these frontiers are quiet. It will be two centuries before migrating hordes of barbarians begin to make their presence felt upon the walls that enclose the civilization of the ancient world.

Christian missionaries went out into a civilization of "one-world." Here was the first element of readiness: a situation in which men could travel speedily and safely over a vast network of roads and waterways that linked town with town all the way from Jerusalem to London, from Gibraltar to the shores of the Black Sea. Not until modern times did Europe and the Near East know anything approaching the ease of travel and communication established by political power of imperial Rome. The way was cleared for the apostolic missionaries.

## THE GRAECO-ROMAN CULTURAL WORLD

If ROMAN power provided the political unity, policed the roads, and kept the peace, what spread over the empire by these means was largely Greek. A thin veneer of Greek culture extended over all the lands bordering the Mediterranean Sea. When a man traveled from Spain to Alexandria, or from Milan to Antioch, he moved everywhere in the familiar atmosphere of Hellenistic culture. The modern world again is growing accustomed to the unifying force of a common culture. For example, the Eskimo in Alaska, the Filipino in the Pacific, or the Brazilian in South America drives a Ford, smokes a Lucky Strike, and looks at movies made in Hollywood. He speaks of democracy. It is *Americanism* which has influenced him. So it was with *Hellenism* in the ancient world. Though Greek influences were more in the realm of ideas than of business or politics, it was this kind of a situation that existed in the Roman Empire.

The thin veneer of Hellenistic culture was just deep enough to provide the Christian missionaries with two invaluable aids: a common language and a common set of ideas.

Whatever his native tongue, nearly everyone in the Mediterranean world had a smattering of the simple Greek into which the language of classical Greece had developed. It was the common speech of the empire. As such it was not only the language in which the New Testament was written, but also the tongue in which the Gospel of Jesus Christ was proclaimed. Christian missionaries everywhere in the apostolic age could make their language understood, and it seemed to them that in this *fulness of time* God had overruled the confusion of tongues dividing men for centuries. As He had once "confounded the language" of those who sought to reach heaven by the Tower of Babel, so now He had prepared the way for those who would know Him in Jesus Christ.

Furthermore, the spread of a common set of ideas, or ways in which men thought, was of immense assistance to the apostles. How important this was is obvious. We know today that one does not preach the Gospel in precisely the same way to a New York congregation, the folk of a Chinese village, or a band of African savages in the hinterland of Liberia. In each case there are different cultures in the background that shape men's understanding and thinking. This cultural background sharply affects the way in which the Christian message is made real and compelling to people. But the task of the first-century missionary was providentially simplified. Everywhere men and women heard and understood the Good News of their redemption in Christ in the same patterns of thought.

## THE PREPARATION IN THE SYNAGOGUES

STILL another element in the world of ideas played its part in this unique readiness for the Gospel. Judaism had already marked out a path around the Mediterranean ahead of Christianity. Dispersed through the centers of the empire were colonies of Jewish merchants and traders, despised by the Romans, yet perhaps for that very reason suffered to maintain their community life and their synagogues with little interference. The religion of these Jews had a strong attraction for the more serious-minded pagans. Jewish monotheistic convictions and high moral standards won respect from earnest men in a day of spiritual decay and moral decline. The strong personal conviction of the Jew that God was concerned with human events and human history appealed to those who could find no ultimate principle of meaning in pagan life. Indeed, the very antiquity of the Jewish faith gave it authority in a world that placed a high value upon things ancient.

As a result, large numbers of Gentiles frequented the Jewish schools and were drawn to the fringes of the synagogues. They may not have been converted in great numbers, but they came to know something of the religion of Israel. They met the Old Testament in its Greek version, absorbing its ethical ideals, catching a glimpse of its hope for the coming of a Messiah. To such Gentiles the Christian proclamation came with great force. The Gospel of a New Covenant, the message of the fulfillment of the Old Testament hope in Jesus the Messiah, fell upon prepared ground in their hearts. It is not surprising that the first Gentile converts to Christianity were those made ready by the missionary spirit of Judaism itself. Even in the synagogues of the dispersed Jews, God's preparation in Old Israel was manifest.

These external conditions—the political unity of the ancient world with its ease of travel and communication, the cultural unity that provided a common language and familiar patterns of thought everywhere, the preparation made by the Jews dispersed throughout the empire—gave force to the Christian conviction that there was a unique readiness for the Gospel at this moment in human history. But equally important was the religious atmosphere of the empire. The spiritual restlessness of the ancient world, too, was part of the *fulness of time*.

### RELIGIOUS PAGANISM

MEN today think of paganism as meaning *without religion*. Much of the paganism of the modern world is irreligious, but this was not the case in the world in which the Early Church found itself. Ancient paganism was religious paganism. One of the most remarkable features of Graeco-Roman life was the religious ferment that pervaded it. People sometimes say of the first century that by this time "the gods of Olympus were dead." It would be more accurate to remark that they had merely once again changed their shapes. No longer appearing, as in the old mythology, to take their capricious pleasures in the world of men, yet the old gods still symbolized the mysterious supernatural forces beyond men's control or understanding.

Moreover, the little domestic deities, the lares and penates of the household, were still the protecting spirits of the family, field, and market place. The Emperor Augustus, seeking to halt the moral decay in Rome's civic and social life, had striven valiantly to recall men to the sturdy virtues of the ancient Roman religion of hearth and harvest deities. He had failed, largely because the primitive religion of the old Roman city-state in the days of the Republic had little appeal to the hordes of different peoples in the immense imperial world. It could hardly serve as an effective bond of unity, for example, between Caesar's Asiatic subjects, inheritors of a thousand years of culture and civilization, and the savage tribesmen of the German forests or the British fens who were the newest Roman provincials.

Thus the religious beliefs and observances of a bygone day exercised little real power in men's hearts. Those few who clung to the old-fashioned virtues found their strength in the ethical ideals of the Stoic philosophers; yet Stoicism, like nearly all that remained of the ancient philosophies, was an evangel for only the highly educated minority. The masses of people in the vast empire, craving escape from the frustrations of life, sought to satisfy their spiritual hunger in the new *mystery religions*. These, at least, spoke a message of personal salvation.

The real religious excitement of the pagan world centered in those cults called collectively mystery religions. As a result of Rome's conquest of the remains of the empire of Alexander the Great in the Near East, the exotic religious movements of the Orient drifted westwards. From Greece, Egypt, Syria, and Asia Minor came these salvation-cults, promising their adherents immortality of some kind, and providing an emotional outlet for thousands of people.

There was a rough similarity among these Eastern religions. In most of them salvation was portrayed in the death and rebirth of a legendary semi-divine hero or saviour-god. The central rite of the mystery was the symbolic initiation of the believer into the immortality conferred upon him by the divine deliverer. Nearly all the mysteries were cults of emotional ecstasy. Some were harmless enough, though with generally little ethical content. Others were so openly erotic that even the tolerant imperial authorities refused to countenance them. But none made exclusive claims upon their adherents. Men were free to seek all the consolations that the religious world offered.

This spiritual hunger of the ancient world was fertile soil upon which the seeds of Christianity could be sown. The climate of religious restlessness was itself part of that *fulness of time* in which the Christian revelation was given. Men were searching for a Gospel of redemption.

Christianity came into little open conflict with these manifestations of pagan religion. It is true that from time to time high-minded pagans sought to revive the ancient philosophies as ways of life, but their limited appeal seldom made them a serious barrier to the spread of the Gospel. In fact, once men trained in the philosophy of antiquity became converted in numbers to the Christian Church, Greek philosophic thought itself was interpreted as a special kind of preparation for the ultimate truth that Christ revealed.

The oriental religious ideas of the mystery cults, on the other hand, were often a menace to the integrity of the Christian faith. The danger did not arise when the Church stood opposed to the array of pagan cults, but rather when men sought to import the ideas behind these cults into Christian thinking. This was the story of the great theological crisis in the Early Church. But before we look at the conflict of doctrine which threatened Christianity, let us turn to the more immediate struggle into which the Church was thrust: the clash with the imperial Roman government.

## CHRIST OR CAESAR?

THE first clash of loyalties came to the early Christians when they were confronted with the demands of the final religion in the Roman world, the official *State Cult*. The one thing which the diverse peoples of the empire had in common was their subjection to the rule of the Caesars. The eagles of the legions cast a long shadow from Scotland to Persia. A single universal political allegiance marked this "one-world."

Seeking to bolster that allegiance with a kind of divine sanction, the Emperor Augustus and his successors gave it religious expression in the imperial State Cult. Though little more than a religion of civil obedience, it demanded that men give their highest loyalty to the State and all for which it stood. The totalitarian state religion was a kind of supercult, to be added to whatever tribal or personal religion a man might have. The design was to provide throughout the empire a bond of spiritual unity, knitting together the various peoples in their highest allegiance. The final altar of the pagan world was this altar of *Roma* and her glory.

The cult of the state naturally centered in the person of the Emperor. He was the living symbol of the protection, peace, and prosperity which the state brought to its citizens, the gifts, so to speak, of the divine *Roma*. This was not emperor worship in the sense that the Caesars were supernatural beings, but it was plainly the worship of the divinity of the state, embodied in its imperial leader.

Here is the tragic situation that has been repeated again and again in the history of mankind: the civic life of a society receiving the idolatrous loyalty of its own citizenry. Here is man making an idol out of the works of his own hands, turning to worship the social and political order that he has built.

The fall of all the great civilizations of the past five thousand years has been presaged by this idolatry. Already it was sapping the spiritual energies of the classical world. When man's own created order of things demands of him the allegiance he can give only to God, then the forces of self-destruction are at work in his civilization. The Roman Empire was already dying. Barbarian invasions did not bring about the decline of Rome. The root cause of decay was that spiritual desolation in which the ancient world could no longer resist man's idolatry of man. The empire in the end worshipped itself to death. Those who have seen this demonic principle again at work are increasingly aware that the last altars of ancient Rome speak with grim warning to the modern world.

But across the centuries the voice of Christian courage speaks with equal clarity. The challenge came to the Church before the first century was ended: *Christ or Caesar?* Which receives man's primary allegiance? Christians perceived that within the State Cult the real enemy of man lurked. The deepest spiritual temptation is not the simple idolatry of ignorance or superstition, but the ultimate idolatry of human pride. The pagan world, aroused to fury by the fearless and stubborn refusal of Christians to participate in the State Cult, poured abuse and scorn upon a people whose watchword was *Thou shalt have none other gods but me.* The charges leveled against the Christians were not what are called religious. They were rather those of a social and political order that saw in Christianity a dangerous and subversive force. The charges were those of disloyalty, lack of patriotism, and denial of civic obligations.

### THE CHURCH OF THE MARTYRS

THE persecution of Christians was the inevitable result of this clash of loyalties. The Church poured out its courageous challenge to the empire in the blood of the martyrs.

Never was this more bravely done than by St. Polycarp, aged Bishop of Smyrna, and grand old man of the Early Church. Dragged before the proconsul in the year 155, Polycarp bore with dignity the taunts and jeers of the mob in the crowded stadium. Before him stood the altar of *Roma;* a pinch of incense dropped in the flame would suffice. The magistrate was not unkind. "Remember your age," he said. "Swear by the divinity of Caesar." Others urged the old man. "What harm is there in saying *Lord* Caesar . . . swear by him . . . curse this Christ."

Polycarp looked at them steadfastly. "Eighty and six years have I served Him and He has done me no wrong. How then can I blaspheme my King who saved me?" And they led him away, like the thousands before and after him who were tortured and burned, stoned by the mobs, torn apart by the wild beasts of the arena, or crucified in imitation of the Lord for whom they died.

We need not trace the persecutions in detail. The first outbreak occurred in Rome when the Emperor Nero sought to lay the blame for the devastating fire of 64 A.D. upon the Christian groups of the city. The last persecution closed in the year 311 when the imperial *Edict of Toleration* acknowledged that Christianity had captured the empire.

In the two hundred and fifty intervening years Christians lived under an ever-present shadow of death. There were moments, even years of respite in one locality or another, but no Christian for six generations was entirely free from the threat of discovery and arrest. Crime need not be alleged against him; membership in the Christian

*Ecclesia* was enough. *Non licet esse vos* was the decree: "It is not lawful for you to exist!"

The early persecutions were local in character, as often the work of unruly mobs as of the magistrates. Nero's persecution, in which St. Peter and St. Paul were martyred, was confined to the capital city, while the outbreak of 175-180 A.D., during the reign of the Emperor Marcus Aurelius, was chiefly felt in Gaul, Asia Minor, and Rome. Similarly, the great persecution of 202 A.D. took the lives of hundreds of Christians, but its heaviest force was exerted in the localities of Egypt and North Africa.

Persecution did little to diminish the zeal of Christians. On the contrary, it heightened their fellowship and increased their sense of mission in the dying ancient world. The expansion of Christian communities continued without pause, and by the middle of the third century the Christian population of the empire was large and influential. Men and women had been drawn to the Church from all classes of society. In many areas the Church now made little pretense of concealment.

**THE LATER PERSECUTIONS**

THE sudden increase of Christian strength in the third century was partly due to the forty years of comparative peace that came to the Church after the persecution of 202 A.D. These first decades of the third century were years when religious bewilderment and cynicism spread widely through the pagan world. Only the Christians held their religious convictions with any intensity. For most men, what seemed good in any religion or philosophy deserved toleration and respect. The private chapel of the

Emperor Alexander Severus symbolized the popular agnostic state of mind. In it were statues of the Greek god Orpheus, Abraham of the Old Testament, the philosophic moralist Apollonius, and Jesus Christ.

But in 249 A.D. the situation abruptly changed. The Emperor Decius, watching the frontiers crumble under increasing pressure from the barbarians of central Europe, and confronted with a severe economic depression in the empire, made a valiant attempt to revive the sturdy spirit of ancient Rome. Perceiving that the real weakness of the empire lay in the decline of its moral and spiritual strength, Decius was convinced that if the glory of Rome were to be recovered it must once again rest upon the ancient virtues of the old Roman religion. The multitude of corrupting and subversive sects, chief among which was Christianity, must be destroyed.

The persecution of Decius fell upon the Church like a thunderbolt. Backed by all the repressive machinery of the government, a determined attempt was made to stamp out Christianity through the whole empire. Christians were arrested by the thousands, especial care being taken to seize the bishops and leaders of the Church. Everywhere men were required to make clear their religious allegiance.

The method of attack of the imperial government revealed its real purpose: not to punish individual Christians, but to break up and destroy the organization of the Christian Church. The magistrates were less interested in making men martyrs than in persuading them to renounce their allegiance to Christ. Apostates, as perhaps the Roman officials knew, would be excluded by Christian discipline from the communion and fellowship of the Church. The greater their number, the greater the disruption of the Christian community. The magistrates, therefore, seem to have made it easy to secure certificates that pagan sacrifice had been offered, and thousands of men and women who had been converted to Christianity during the forty years of peace could not now face the stern obligations of ultimate loyalty to Jesus Christ.

The imperial policy of encouraging apostasy created such chaos in the life of the Church that the Decian persecution came within a narrow margin of destroying the Christian organization. Only the wise decision of bishops like Cyprian of Carthage and Cornelius of Rome averted a catastrophe. They made a daring modification in the strict penitential discipline of the Church, receiving back with forgiveness those whose weakness had led them into apostasy.

Fortunately, the severe trial of the Church during the reign of Decius was of short duration. The emperor was killed on the frontier in the year 251 while leading his troops against the Goths, and under his successors the persecution gradually died out. After 260 A.D. peace descended upon the Church for another forty-year period, until the final imperial persecution of Christianity just before the accession of the Emperor Constantine.

### DIVISION IN THE CHRISTIAN RANKS

DURING the confusion of the Decian persecution, the bishops' decision to relax the harsh discipline of the Church, admitting back into fellowship those who had committed the sin of apostasy, did not pass unchallenged. An able and high-minded presbyter of the community at

Rome named Novatian, sternly rigorous in his view of the requirements of Christian obedience, led a small party in violent opposition to the merciful policy of Cyprian and Cornelius. It seemed to Novatian and his followers that the extension of forgiveness to apostates made nonsense out of the high moral demands of Jesus for unswerving loyalty and self-sacrifice. Had thousands of Christians suffered martyrdom in vain, only to have the weak-hearted forgiven their cowardice? To the puritanical Novatians the absolute challenge of the Gospel was unmistakably clear.

The outcome of the controversy was the separation of Novatian and his party from communion with the great body of the Church. This *Novatian Schism,* as it is called, lingered to plague the Early Church for over a century. A similar dispute arose in 313 A.D., after the last persecution under the Emperor Diocletian had failed in its repetition of the attempt to destroy the Church. Again the separatist group was impatient of the weakness shown by many under the strain of persecution. Led by a rigorist named Donatus, they withdrew to claim for themselves the name of the only true Catholic Church. Like the Novatians, the Donatists maintained their organization, though confined to North Africa, for nearly two centuries.

The existence of the Novatians and the Donatists provoked a conscious decision concerning the nature of the Christian Church. Both schismatic groups showed a tendency to regard the Church as the "society of the elect" rather than a fellowship for the redemption of sinners. However much the courageous stand of the separatists for an absolute principle evokes admiration, the early Fathers were right in their decision that there is no human sin beyond God's forgiveness, a forgiveness which is found within the brotherhood of His children here and now. The withdrawn "fellowship of the righteous," gathering its members around one absolute demand, has lost sight of the Church as the essential community of all men in Christ where the redemptive power of God operates on saint and sinner alike.

## THE CONFLICT WITH PAGAN THEOLOGY

THE gravest menace to Christianity in the ancient world was not, however, the frontal attack of pagan persecution. This, at least, could be resisted openly. Far more dangerous was the subtle penetration of Christian thinking with pagan religious ideas. As the ranks of the Church were swelled by thousands of converts drawn from the different races and peoples of the Mediterranean world, pagan notions were carried over with them into men's understanding of God's revelation in Jesus Christ. The general tendency of these ideas was to separate the Gospel events from their historical setting, surrounding the story of the life and death and resurrection of Jesus with the mythological atmosphere of the mystery religions. Here was an attempt to substitute for the mighty acts of God in human history a kind of legendary religious fairy tale in which the old pagan notions of divinity could still exist.

The most serious theological crisis of this character that confronted the primitive Church was the assimilation of Christianity to a popular speculative system known as *Gnosticism*.[3] The Gnostic philosopher pictured the world

---

[3] From the Greek word *gnosis*, knowledge. The Gnostics pretended to a secret knowledge, possession of which enabled man to be saved.

as the battleground of two opposing divine forces, one good, the other evil, powers that were perpetually at war both in this world and in men's hearts. The forces of good were spiritual; those of evil were material. This kind of dualism invaded Christianity, attempting to make the Christian revelation a vehicle for its mythological ideas.

The Gnostic, for example, refused to believe that the world, being material and therefore evil, could have been brought into being by the supreme good God. It must have been the creation of a lesser deity, and he pointed triumphantly to the Old Testament as showing this opposing creator-god at work, imprisoning the souls of men in the physical world of flesh and matter. In the New Testament the Gnostic saw a more powerful divine being, the saviour messenger of the good God, at work to free men's spirits from the evil material creation in which they are caught. This is the real meaning of the work of Jesus Christ, said the Gnostic. He is the messenger of the eternal and ultimate Spirit who brings to men the saving knowledge of the true nature of good and evil. As men receive this knowledge so they are saved from the bondage of the created world. Salvation came through enlightenment, not through the response of faith.

To the Gnostic, of course, Jesus could not have been truly human, for the messenger of the supreme spiritual God could not have entered the evil physical world in a body of flesh and blood. Their doctrine was that Jesus only *seemed* to have a human body. He did not really hunger and thirst, suffer and die; He only appeared to do so in a kind of divine masquerade. The result was to make Jesus just another godling, to strip Him of all humanity, and to deny Him any identification with men. This makes nonsense out of the central affirmation of Christian faith and experience that the Son of God was made flesh in Jesus of Nazareth, assuming the frailty of man's humanity that in His victory over human sin men might share His eternal life. In the end, the Gnostic speculations make nonsense out of monotheism as well, turning Christianity into just another polytheistic system.

Moreover, Gnosticism threatened the moral imperative of Christianity as well as its biblical and historical revelation. Man in this system is not saved from sin, that is, his own denial of the relationship with God for which he was created. Instead, man is saved from the bondage of flesh, a concept that allowed the Gnostic to deny all claims of the flesh on one hand, or to indulge all the desires of the body on the other. If no essential relation could exist between man's body and his spirit, then extreme asceticism or gross immorality were alternate ways of life.

Gnosticism degenerated into a number of absurdities, perhaps the worst being that of a sect called the *Ophites,* or snake-worshippers. Their use of Scripture reveals how the Gnostics wrested the meaning of the Bible to their purposes. Did not the serpent persuade Adam and Eve to eat of the tree of knowledge? Was this not the first step taken in the enlightenment of man concerning the dualism of good and evil? The serpent, therefore, must have been a heavenly messenger sent to start men along the path of freedom from bondage to the material world of the creator-god. Indeed, the serpent of the Garden of Eden and the Saviour of the New Testament were actually the same heavenly being in different forms. Surely, claimed the

Ophite, this is what Jesus meant when He said *As Moses lifted up the serpent in the wilderness, even so must the Son of man be lifted up!*

Ridiculous as this seems today, the Gnostic threat in the Early Church was serious in character and extent.

## THE NATURE OF THE THEOLOGICAL CRISIS

GNOSTICISM posed as the "enlightened science" of the ancient world, and its impact upon Christianity was basically an attempt to adjust the Christian revelation to its own ideas. In some ways that is an ever-present temptation to the generations of men. The science of the ancient world was a cosmology of polytheism. Hence, Jesus is made over into a mythical being in this divine hierarchy. But this same temptation has been at work in more recent history. The science of the nineteenth century involved a doctrine of man's progress and the gradual evolution of perfection. Hence, Jesus so often appeared in writings of a generation or two ago as the perfect human being, the kind of superman into which it was the destiny of all men to grow. There may seem little in common between the Gnostic speculations of nearly two thousand years ago and the humanistic ideals of yesterday, but the impact upon Christian thinking was similar.

The Gnostics boasted themselves the possessors of a secret revelation of their saving knowledge, imparted by Jesus to select disciples, and passed on from them to their successors in the inner Gnostic circles. This secret knowledge was the true Gospel. Gnostic propaganda was continuous; Gnostic writings flooded the Church. Their literature took the form of rewriting and adjusting the books of

25

Scripture to their purposes, as well as supplying additional "gospels" and "acts of the apostles" that made the principles of Gnosticism seem the true interpretation of Christianity.

The early Fathers of the Church rose to defend the faith from these devastating attacks upon the heart of the Christian revelation. The martyrs of the Roman stadium were the spectacular heroes of the primitive Church, but no less heroic was the work of the early Christian theologians. Theirs was the task of answering man's ultimate questions about God and about himself, and doing it without sacrificing the difficult truths of the Christian Gospel to the easy solutions of pagan religion. St. Ignatius of Antioch, St. Irenaeus the Bishop of Lyons, Justin Martyr the Christian philosopher, Clement of Alexandria the brilliant Christian teacher, all fought and won a battle on the field of theology quite as decisive for the survival of the Gospel of Jesus Christ as was the victory of the martyrs and saints on the field of conflict with the imperial government.

### THE INSTITUTIONS OF THE EARLY CHURCH

INEVITABLY, the impact of pagan thought in the form of Gnosticism affected the institutional life of the Early Church. Before the middle of the second century there was little development of fixed and authoritative institutional forms in which the life of the Church was embodied. Primitive Christian creeds, for example, were only the briefest pledges of acceptance of Jesus Christ as Lord. The ministry of the Church existed in a wide variety of patterns, underneath which only the main outline of the threefold order was discernible. The books of the New Testament were not yet gathered into an authoritative canon of Holy Scripture.

In the face of the dangerous Gnostic pressure that threatened to make over the Christian revelation into another polytheistic system, the development of authoritative institutions within which the Gospel was protected and enshrined was both natural and necessary. Christian thought speedily turned to define the so-called *Institutions* of the Ancient Catholic Church. Creed, Ministry, and New Testament Scriptures alike assumed a fixed form.

It used to be said that this institutional crystallization in the second century was essentially foreign to the spirit of the New Testament. Men interpreted it as a kind of hard protective shell thrown around the Christian revelation, perhaps unavoidable at the time, but ultimately having a narrowing and paralyzing effect upon man's recognition of the operation of the Holy Spirit. Thus a century ago many Christian scholars were advocating the repudiation of these institutional shackles of human devising and a return to the untrammeled simplicities of the "religion of Jesus."

Today it is understood again that there are no such simplicities. The roots of the Church's institutions lie deeply embedded in the earliest strand of the Gospel itself.[4] Instead of a protective shell applied to Christianity at the point of its contact with the world, these structural forms of the Church are actually the internal living skeleton of the Christian organism, fundamental to its life, growth, and purpose in the plan of God. The seeds of the institutions of the Christian Church were there from the

---

[4] See the discussion of New Testament Church life in *The Holy Scriptures,* ch. x.

beginning; their development was merely hastened by
the external pressures of the pagan world.

## THE APPEAL TO APOSTOLIC TRADITION

THE chief antagonist of the Gnostics among the western
Christian Fathers in the second century was St. Irenaeus.
Born in Smyrna around the year 135, he came to Gaul,
where he was eventually made bishop of the Christian
community in the town of Lyons. Writing in the last
quarter of the second century, Irenaeus made a vigorous
and decisive refutation of Gnosticism.

Against the claims to a secret *gnosis* handed down to a
chosen few, Irenaeus appealed to the great body of well-
known Christian teaching that had been preserved and
openly proclaimed everywhere by the apostles and their
successors. Never had there been the slightest trace of
apostolic authority for the Gnostic views. Here Irenaeus
stood on firm ground. Did he not himself learn the Christian tradition from Polycarp who had actually known the
apostles? Had he not heard Polycarp condemn the Gnostics? How could anyone be led astray by Gnostic claims
when it was an obvious fact that in none of the Christian
communities founded by the apostles themselves had any
secret *gnosis* even been proclaimed?

Irenaeus made much of his appeal to the public teaching
of the churches of apostolic foundation. In these widely
separated communities all over the Mediterranean world
the same faith was simultaneously proclaimed. In each one
of them an unbroken succession of known bishops and
teachers had guarded and transmitted the tradition received from Jesus' own companions. Here is the *apostolic*

*succession* to which the second-century Fathers appealed. What was first emphasized was not the succession of sacramental ministers in which the sacerdotal power of the Christian ministry is preserved, but rather a succession of authorized teachers, chosen to guard and proclaim the *Apostolic Teaching* or *Tradition*. Thus the purity of Christian teaching anywhere may be tested by its agreement with the received traditions of faith in the great churches of apostolic foundation.

In a later generation this concept of apostolic succession revealed a different primary emphasis. Where is the true Church? The Fathers of the second century had no hesitancy in replying "Where the Apostolic Tradition is found." But as that tradition was guaranteed by an official succession of ministers, the answer soon became "Where the apostolic succession is found." And so it came about that apostolic succession was attached both to the preservation of the true faith and to the continuance of a properly ordained sacramental ministry in the life of the Church.

It was in the days of Irenaeus that the Fathers appealed also to the authoritative New Testament Scriptures. The canon of the New Testament books as it is now was in process of formation.

## THE CANON OF NEW TESTAMENT SCRIPTURES

THE second-century world abounded with Christian writings of the kind in the New Testament. At least a half-dozen "gospels" were circulated in addition to the four included in the New Testament, many of them being pious attempts to fill the gaps left by the Evangelists in the story of the life of Jesus. An *Infancy Gospel,* for example contained a number of charming, though wholly inappropriate stories of Jesus' boyhood. Similarly, numerous books of "acts of the apostles" described events in the travels of those apostles whom the *Acts* does no more than mention.

Much of this body of legendary and imaginative literature reflected the Gnostic interpretation of the Christian revelation. Moreover, even the authentic Christian books were subjected to expurgation and reinterpretation by Gnostic teachers interested in gathering together a set of sacred writings that would give the color of authority to their teachings.

Confronted by the array of pious legend mixed with genuine apostolic writings, and aroused by the Gnostic selection of scriptures, the Church formed the canon of true New Testament Scripture. By the end of the second century the authoritative books were much as they are today. The method of determination of authentic Scripture was simple, and along the lines already suggested in the appeal of Irenaeus. Was a writing in conformity with the received Apostolic Tradition? Was a book of undoubted apostolic authorship, or written by a companion of the apostles? Did a book possess the endorsement of an ancient Christian community of apostolic foundation?

By these three tests the claim of a Christian writing to be Holy Scripture was judged. Those books that form the New Testament are the writings that in the mind of the Early Church fulfilled the requirements, and thus were regarded as Holy Scriptures wherein the Apostolic Tradition was set forth in its clearest and purest form. Hence the New Testament has always been the place of primary appeal in matters of Christian faith and life.

MAN is always trying to make intelligible his experience of God. Theology is no more than the attempt to do this, and each man who tries to interpret his religious experience is inescapably a theologian, however simple or profound he may be. By the same necessity the early Christians became theologians.

The Gospel did not consist of discourses on Christian doctrine. It recorded simply what the first Christians believed to be the mighty acts of God, performed in Jesus Christ for man's deliverance from sin and death, and it portrayed vividly the effect of those acts upon the men among whom He lived and died and rose from the dead. The immediate concern of the primitive Church was the proclamation of these mighty events, the Good News of Salvation. Christians were first "witnesses of the resurrection" and missionaries of the Gospel. Theological explanation and interpretation came afterwards.

But just as Gnostic pressure speeded the development of the institutional life of the Christian community, so also it stirred Christian teachers to explore the meaning of God's action in human history and its implications for man. If the speculations of the Gnostics threatened to overwhelm the Christian revelation with the old polytheism, what were the true answers to the questions raised about God and man, about Christ and the world?

The central problem of the early Christian theologians was the question of *the purpose and activity of God*. The answer that they gave arose from their experience of redemption in Christ. The experience came first; theological formulation tried to make that experience intelligible.

The answer that Christian theology gave to the problem of the purpose and activity of God was the assertion of *Incarnation*. The overwhelming experience of Christianity was that man walks closest to God when he is in the company of the Living Christ, and the presence of that Divine Companion is inseparable from the historical person of Jesus of Nazareth. The New Testament writers knew that "God was in Christ," *The Word was made flesh*—or, as the Nicene Creed says, . . . *Jesus Christ, the only-begotten Son of God . . . Who for us men and our salvation came down from heaven . . . And was made man.*

This Incarnation (a word that means simply "becoming flesh") of the Son of God is for the Christian the central act of all history. Indeed, it is the event that stamps history with God's meaning. Men did not come to believe the Incarnation because they constructed a picture of a God who was capable of this act. On the contrary, they came to believe reluctantly and with difficulty, because nothing else could explain their experience that in the company of Jesus of Nazareth they found companionship with the Living God.

The affirmation of *The Word made flesh* left some deep questions for Christian theology to answer: How is the Incarnate Son related to God the Father? And what of God the Holy Spirit? How preserve the essential unity of God and yet speak of Him in three Persons? Furthermore, how can we speak of Jesus Christ as God *and* Man? How can the perfect humanity of Jesus be asserted in the same breath which affirms Him to be Incarnate Son of God? [5]

---

[5] These problems of Christian theology are discussed at length in the volume in this series entitled *The Faith of the Church*. Here the questions are merely raised at the appropriate place in the history of the Church.

From the middle of the second century onwards a long procession of Christian Fathers wrestled with these questions: Tertullian, Cyprian, and Augustine in the West; Origen, Basil, Athanasius, Gregory of Nyssa, Gregory of Nazianzus, and others in the East. Slowly the Christian doctrine of the Trinity took shape, the doctrine of God-in-three-Persons, "One in substance, power, and eternity" and yet Father, Son, and Holy Spirit. It was framed in men's minds because nothing else was adequate to describe the mighty acts of God that laid hold upon men in their religious experience. Slowly, too, *Christology*, the doctrine of the nature and person of Christ, was expressed in terms that at once affirmed Christ as the Incarnate Son of God and yet maintained the full and complete humanity of the Man of Nazareth.

## THE CREEDS OF THE CHURCH

INEVITABLY, in seeking to answer the questions raised by the affirmation of God's activity in Incarnation, half-truths were seized upon from time to time. When tested against the full Christian experience of God these proved to be inadequate. Ultimately such half-truths bore the name of *heresy*, but it must be remembered that in a day before the doctrines of orthodoxy were clearly defined, heresy was often simply the honest search of the zealous teacher for some adequate expression of truth.

The Church early rejected the teaching that Jesus was so much the best and holiest of men that God conferred upon Him the Divine Sonship, or "adopted" Him, so to speak. The idea that Jesus grew into divinity or became divine neither satisfied Christian experience, nor was it the witness of the Apostolic Tradition. Men might be called "sons of God" by adoption; Christ was that by nature. *Adoptionism,* as this point of view was later called, was considered a heresy, but it is well to remember that at the outset, those who advanced this idea were endeavoring to make intelligible the unique relation between God and Jesus Christ without imperiling the principle of monotheism.

On the other hand, any explanation of the person of Jesus that lost sight of His complete humanity was equally unsatisfactory and incompatible with the Christian revelation. Jesus was not simply God in a temporary human disguise. He was Man *and* God, and it was the task of making this basic conviction of Christian religious experience clear that presented the Early Church with its crucial theological challenge.

As the mind of the Church moved slowly towards the final theological formularies of what later were accepted as orthodoxy, men began to affirm their faith in credal form. The creeds were not explanations of the mysteries of God's acts among men, but rather proclamations of the historical events in which God revealed Himself through the life and death and resurrection of Jesus. They are not primarily a series of theological propositions about God to which men are required to give intellectual assent. The credal affirmations testify to the historical acts in which God revealed Himself. They proclaim the Gospel, and call men to a personal self-commitment to Him who has thus acted in Christ for us and for our salvation.

The earliest credal professions of faith, probably made by converts to Christianity at the moment of baptism, are contained in the primary strands of the Apostolic Tradition. *I believe that Jesus Christ is the Son of God* is the credal profession made by the Ethiopian eunuch in *Acts* 8:37 at the moment of his baptism by Philip. Here is the simplest credal form, the acceptance of Jesus as God's Messiah and man's Saviour. There are signs of such primitive confessions of the Christian faith in a dozen places in the New Testament.

The natural elaboration of credal forms was accelerated by the impact of Gnostic speculation. It was necessary for the Christian community to guard its historical revelation against both semi-pagan interpretations and inadequate explanations of the person and work of Christ. For example, confronted with the attempt to strip Jesus of His essential humanity and make Him just another godling, the creed answered with vigorous insistence upon the reality of His human nature. Hence the phrases *Born of the Virgin Mary; suffered under Pontius Pilate; was crucified, dead, and buried. . . .* Even now Christians still confess their faith in a creed that dates the mighty historical acts of God in the governorship of an obscure Roman provincial administrator, Pontius Pilate. They are proclaiming historical events and facts of the Gospel, not theological notions and speculations.

The *Apostles' Creed* was finally fixed as it is today in the middle of the eighth century, but long before that its general form had taken shape. By the end of the third century similar creeds were in use all over Christendom as baptismal confessions, and only minor changes in language produced the final Apostles' Creed. If it is no longer necessary to accept the legend that this creed received its name

35

because it was composed by the apostles themselves, it is still apostolic in the sense that it proclaims those acts of God which form the Good News of the Gospel of Jesus Christ.

## THE THEOLOGICAL COUNCILS

THE *Nicene Creed* is a later and more deliberate composition than the Apostles' Creed. After the recognition of Christianity by the Emperor Constantine, with the resulting freedom and protection granted the Church by the imperial government, the Christian Fathers sought guidance in their theological task through the activity of great assemblies of bishops and leaders. These were the ecumenical (worldwide) councils of the fourth and fifth centuries.

Men gradually accepted the idea that the mind of the Church could be both informed and expressed through the decisions of proper representatives gathered from every quarter, deliberating under the guidance of the Holy Spirit. While considerable controversy accompanied this conciliar activity, the decisions of the great councils in the end won the support of Christendom. To a large degree the formularies of these councils of the undivided Early Church have been an authoritative court of appeal in Christian doctrinal disputes ever since.

The Nicene Creed is the elaborate profession of faith which has come down from this age of conciliar decision. At the *Council of Nicaea* in the year 325 the Fathers rejected the doctrine that Christ was a kind of intermediate semi-divine being, neither fully God nor completely man. This was the teaching of Arius, a presbyter of the Church at Alexandria. Perceiving that such a notion opened the door to admit polytheism into Christianity, a heroic defense of the integrity of the principle of incarnation was conducted by Athanasius, Bishop of Alexandria. Today the Nicene Creed vividly reflects this controversy in its insistent phrases describing Christ as *God of God, Light of Light . . . Begotten, not made . . . Being of one substance with the Father . . . Who for us men and for our salvation came down from heaven, and was incarnate . . . And was made man . . .* He is none other than Incarnate God.

The controversy over Arianism lasted until the second ecumenical *Council of Constantinople* in 381 A.D. It was then that the mind of the Chruch was turned to the problem of describing how the divine and human natures could exist simultaneously in Jesus Christ without destroying the integrity of His Person.

The *Council of Ephesus* in 431 A.D., and the *Council of Chalcedon* twenty years later, both addressed themselves to this difficult theological task. The final formula of orthodoxy was expressed at the latter Council: *Therefore, following the holy fathers, we all with one accord teach men to acknowledge . . . our Lord Jesus Christ . . . truly God and truly man . . . of one substance with the Father as regards His Godhead, and at the same time of one substance with us as regards His manhood . . . recognized in two natures, without confusion, without separation, not as parted into two persons, but one and the same Son . . .* He was both God *and* Man. The statement of Chalcedon perhaps did little to explain the mystery of the Incarnation, but it did affirm that permanent and central Christian conviction which theology endeavors in each generation to make intelligible and compelling to men.

## THE DEVELOPMENT OF THE MINISTRY

IN OUR brief glance at the life of the New Testament Church, we have already glimpsed the kind of ministry to which Jesus entrusted His work in the continuing life of His Fellowship.[6] At the end of the first century, the outlines of a threefold ministry were clear.

The first order of ministers, to use a later term, was the *apostolate*. Consisting not only of the original Twelve who had been intimately associated with Jesus, but also of others to whom the responsibility was extended as the Gentile mission required a larger group of leaders, this apostolate was the essential, authoritative ministry in the Christian Fellowship. Its members had received the commission of the Lord Himself. He had clothed them with His authority and charged them with His own ministry. The conviction of the primitive Church regarding the apostles' ministry was expressed in *St. John* 20:21 where the story of the appearance of Jesus to the disciples on the evening of His resurrection contains this charge: *As my Father hath sent me, even so send I you. And when he had said this, he breathed upon them, and saith unto them, Receive ye the Holy Ghost. . . .*

Thus at the heart of the Christian ministry is the apostolate, empowered by the Risen Lord and exercising His own ministry of reconciliation among men. The notable characteristic is the universality of the apostles' ministerial power and responsibility. They exercised a non-localized,

---

[6] See *The Holy Scriptures,* ch. viii.

traveling, missionary ministry, possessing authority everywhere in the Christian world. They were not the ministers of local congregations, but the governors and evangelists of the whole Church.

Oversight of local congregations established by the apostles was entrusted by them to another group of ministers, the *elders*.[7] A body of these elders or presbyters was formed and ordained for the governance of each local Christian community. While the New Testament gives no clear picture of the first setting-apart of such elders, it is plain that the apostles ordained such ministers in imitation of the boards of elders who governed the local Jewish communities with which the first Christians were familiar. In distinction to the apostolate, the ministry of the elders was subordinate and purely local in character. Everywhere the elders deferred to the authority of the apostles when these traveling missionary leaders moved throughout the local churches that made up the whole body of Christendom. Unity in the separated congregations of the Christian Fellowship was symbolized in the single, universal apostolate.

The third order of ministers was another local ministry, that of the *deacons*. They had their origin in the group of men ordained by the apostles in the Jerusalem Church to administer the charity, and care for the poor of the Christian community. This office spread naturally throughout the Church as new congregations were formed during the Gentile mission, and shortly each local church had its group of assisting deacons as well as its governing body of elders.

---

[7] In Greek, *presbuteroi*, whence comes our word *presbyters*.

When the New Testament period closes, this outline of a threefold Church order is clearly discernible: the universal authoritative apostolate, the local elders and deacons. Other, and perhaps temporary, ministries of the first generation of Christianity are disappearing. The permanent threefold structure of the historic Christian ministry remains.

## THE OFFICE OF THE BISHOP

TODAY the historic threefold ministry is known under the names of bishop, priest (or presbyter), and deacon. At some time early in the second century the powers of the universal apostolate began to be exercised locally by a single minister henceforth called the bishop.[8] To him the functions of the apostles were transferred as the apostolate became localized in the episcopate.

There was no doubt at all in the mind of the Early Church that the bishops were the "successors of the apostles," but precisely how this change was effected has always been a problem for historians. The surviving evidence which gives any clear picture of Church life between the years 100 and 150 is scanty and capable of interpretation in different ways. Some scholars, for example, have held that the apostles in the course of time simply disappeared from the scene. The natural consequence was the elevation of one of the elders to exercise the same kind of oversight that a visiting apostle formerly had. This development would be hastened in the early second century by the crystallization of all the Church's institutions in the face of both the Gnostic threat and the hostility

---

[8] From the Greek *episkopos*, meaning overseer or governor.

of the imperial government. Some would further maintain that this elevation of a single minister took place under the direction of the last surviving apostles. It would thus have apostolic sanction, perhaps many of the first bishops being appointed and ordained by the last apostles.

Other scholars have found the origin of the bishop's office not in the elevation of an elder, but in the localization of a member of the apostolate. The gradual settlement of apostolic leaders is seen as a natural process. Their successors in local authority were known as bishops, and the episcopal office was thus formed not out of the presbyterate by elevation, but out of the apostolate by localization.

It is unnecessary to discuss in detail the difficulties in the way of any rigid theory purporting to account for this change in Church order. Any single reconstruction of the manner in which the episcopate inherited the functions of the apostolate will probably not apply to the experience of every Christian congregation in the primitive Church. The important historical fact is that by 150 A.D. this change had taken place in all the widely separated churches of the empire, and everywhere the functions of the apostolate were exercised by bishops. It is, after all, the functions of the essential apostolic ministry empowered by the Lord Himself that are vital to the life of His Church. These functions were transferred to the episcopal order in some historical experience every detail of which perhaps can never fully be recovered. For nearly fifteen hundred years no one questioned the essentially apostolic character of the bishop's ministry. He was the center of the life of the local church; through him the local congregation found its unity with the whole Christian Fellowship.

## THE GREAT CHURCHES OF THE EMPIRE

GENERAL organization was of slow growth among the early Christian communities that had been established by the apostolic missionaries in the cities and towns along the vast network of Roman roads and waterways. At first the unity of all the churches was not one of organization, but of their common faith in Christ. A constant interchange of letters kept them in touch with one another. The evangelists and apostolic delegates who traveled from church to church were the human links in the chain of common allegiance that bound them together.

Gradually each urban Christian community, under the leadership of its bishop, became a center for the evangelization of the smaller towns and country districts surrounding it. At first the new congregations in this missionary expansion were closely linked with the original Christian group. The bishop was still chief pastor and Father-in-God to all his people, and their unity in one family was sometimes symbolized in the consecrated elements sent from his Eucharist in the central church to the altars of outlying groups of the faithful.

With the enormous increase in the number of Christians after the persecutions ended, this primitive organization became inadequate to care for the pastoral needs of the multiplying congregations. More and more the bishop delegated his sacramental ministry and pastoral responsibilities to his assisting presbyters, who in turn began to assume the full duties of parish priests in the local congregations. The result was something like what is known today as the parochial system. At the same time, the bishop found himself concerned with an ever-increasing administrative burden in the care of all the churches within the area that soon became his *diocese.*

Quite naturally, the developed organization of the Church was framed on the model of the civil administrative system of the Roman Empire, a development that was extremely rapid after the recognition of Christianity by the Emperor Constantine. Groups of dioceses in the same region of the imperial world came together, first in an informal manner to deal with common problems, and then in a more organized fashion to form a *province.* The bishop of the chief Christian community in that region, assuming a place of leadership, was later known as the archbishop or metropolitan.[9] While in theory in the Early Church all bishops were regarded as equal in status, in practice it was inevitable that those in the important centers of the empire exercised great influence, and in time, actual jurisdiction over the neighboring areas.

## THE PATRIARCHATES

A FINAL step in the organization of the Early Church was the emergence of the great patriarchal centers in those large cities of the empire where the earliest Christian communities had been of apostolic foundation. Jerusalem, after its final destruction by the Romans in the second century, ceased to be the natural center of Christianity. In-

---

[9] The word *metropolis* means literally mother-city, and the bishop of the chief or central city is naturally the *metropolitan. Archbishop* means simply ruling-bishop, but the early title was one denoting honor rather than power over his brother bishops.

stead, Antioch in Syria, Alexandria in Egypt, and Rome in the western Mediterranean became the main centers of the Church's organization. Gradually acquiring the designation of *Patriarchs,* the bishops of those cities were the foremost clerics of Christendom.[10]

The growth of the large patriarchates in the Early Church was not wholly a matter of administration and organization. The regional divisions reflected the cultural and racial divisions of the Mediterranean world. Antioch was thus the natural center of Syrian Christianity; Alexandria, of Egyptian Christianity. Rome, on the other hand, became expressive of the whole spirit of western Christianity. Greek Christianity received its own center when Constantine moved the seat of imperial administration from Italy to the meeting-place of Europe and Asia Minor on the shores of the Black Sea, the new city of Constantinople. There the fourth and last of the great patriarchates was somewhat belatedly established.

The centuries following the recognition of Christianity were years of intense rivalry among the patriarchates. Antioch, Alexandria, and Constantinople struggled bitterly for precedence in the East. As long as that conflict lasted, Rome, the sole patriarchate in the West, found its own claims to primacy in Christendom unchallenged. But when Constantinople had established its supremacy over Eastern Christendom, the two imperial cities embarked upon a long contest for preëminence in the Church, a struggle that ended only in the final schism between the East and the West in 1054.

---

[10] *Patriarch* means literally ruling-father, an idea which could be expressed in the more common word *pope* (literally father). Hence in the Early Church the name *pope* is not confined to the Bishop of Rome.

The rivalries which marred the relationships between the patriarchates were not due simply to ecclesiastical politics. Christianity was finding indigenous expression among the peoples of the different regions of the empire. The conflicting customs, usages, and ways of thinking that characterized the various greater churches were partly the result of widely different cultural backgrounds. The speculative, philosophic, and theological approach of Greek Christianity, for example, was totally foreign to the practical, moral, and legal genius of Roman Christianity. In some measure the final rupture between the *Orthodoxy* of Constantinople and the *Catholicism* of Rome was less the result of ecclesiastical quarrels than it was the inevitable outcome of the clash of incompatible cultures.

## ROME IN THE EARLY CHURCH

IN VIEW of the important part Rome has played in the history of the Church, something must be said of its rise to eminence in the early centuries. In the first place, the Roman Church did not become important because its bishops were the successors of St. Peter, to whom Jesus was supposed to have given supreme authority over all His followers. The contrary was true. The Roman bishop became an important figure because of the eminence to which the Christian community in Rome attained. There is no shred of evidence that the Bishops of Rome in the first years of the Church's life made any claim to authority because of a commission given by the Lord to St. Peter. That appeal does not appear before the middle of the third century, and does not receive its developed form until the days of the medieval papacy.

Very early, however, the Roman Church assumed a position of leadership in the West. A number of reasons account for this. As the Church of the capital city of the Roman world, it attracted thousands of Christians. All roads led to Rome in the ancient world, and this was as true for the faithful as it was for the pagan. Moreover, a tradition of apostolic foundation gave a Christian community special status and prestige when the apostolic age had passed. Quite naturally, more deference was paid to a Church that claimed, as Rome did, a double apostolic heritage. The Roman community had been the scene of the final labors and the martyrdom of both St. Peter and St. Paul.

The Roman Christian community was the one apostolic foundation in the western Mediterranean world. Eastwards, Ephesus, Antioch, Alexandria, and others were the apostolic centers from which the surrounding areas were evangelized. In the West it was through Rome alone that all the Christian communities of Spain, Gaul, Italy, and much of North Africa looked toward the rest of Christendom. Throughout half the empire no Christian fellowship could challenge the prestige of Rome.

The unique position of the pope, or Bishop of Rome, in the West was greatly enhanced early in the fourth century when the Emperor Constantine moved the seat of his government from the ancient city on the Tiber to Constantinople, the new settlement on the shores of the Bosphorus. Tradition dies hard. For nearly five hundred years the ancient world had looked toward Rome, the Eternal City. As the move to Constantinople coincided with the victory of Christianity in the empire, the Christian world continued to look Romewards. In terms of prestige the "mantle of the Caesars" fell upon the shoulders of the pope.

No catalog of the causes of the natural growth of Rome to a position of primacy would be complete without a tribute to the moral greatness of Roman leadership in the Early Church. Before the first century was over, Roman Christians had displayed their sense of responsibility toward other Christian local churches. This vocation to "the care of all the churches" was faithfully and continuously discharged during the difficult years of the first three centuries. Again, throughout the periods of theological controversy and conflict that marked the life of the Early Church, it was the Roman community which invariably stood fast for decisions ultimately accepted by the whole Church as right and in accord with the Gospel. However much accidents of history helped to increase the influence of the Church of Rome, in the end its early primacy was well-deserved, resting finally upon the character of its Christian leadership.

This is not, however, to say that the primacy of honor won by Rome in these first centuries warranted the later claims of power and supremacy made by the popes of the Middle Ages. The Bishop of Rome in the ancient Church might be first among his equals; he was never the ecclesiastical overlord and ruler of all Christendom that a later age made him.

## CONSTANTINE AND CHRISTIANITY

THE last years of the Early Church begin with the final persecution of Christians by the imperial government early in the fourth century. The Emperor Diocletian was persuaded in 303 A.D. to make another attempt to destroy the power of the Christian institution, and for nearly a decade a persecution similar to the earlier one of Decius raged intermittently throughout the Roman world. The effect of the conflict was to make plain the strength of Christianity. Already the empire had been won; the Church could not be broken. In the year 311 Galerius, the successor of Diocletian in the eastern portion of the empire, conceded defeat in his *Edict of Toleration*. At long last the Church won legal recognition.

But events moved swiftly toward more than mere recognition of Christianity as just another licensed religion. The Emperor Constantine, who had become sole master of the empire in the conflict between contenders for the imperial power following Diocletian's reign, had a clear vision of the magnitude of the task that confronted him. The crumbling imperial world needed, above all, to recover a basic spiritual unity. With acute perception, Constantine realized that Christianity alone could provide this bond of faith. Already the Church had so deeply penetrated the fabric of the empire that it was fast becoming the single universal allegiance of these last years of the ancient world.

Constantine became the imperial patron of Christianity. The *Edict of Milan* of 313 A.D., in which he ratified the earlier decree of Galerius, not only accorded complete and unconditional recognition of Christianity, but also its provisions for compensation and restitution made it plain that the Church was to enjoy the special protection of the imperial government.

Constantine's motives are difficult to see clearly. Certainly at the outset he desired the assistance of Christianity in the task of holding together an empire and a culture which showed unmistakable signs of decay and disintegration. All his life he showed a special sense of responsibility and leadership in Christian affairs. If this was based upon his conviction that an emperor was still *Pontifex Maximus* to his Christian subjects as he had been to his pagan people, it was none the less true that he reigned as a Christian Caesar, a dazzling sight to those who for generations had lived under the terrible shadow of persecution and martyrdom. And if the spectacle of a Christian protector, arrayed in the crown and purple of imperial splendor, was the symbol of the Church's external strength, the sight of the same protector on his death bed, laying aside the royal robes to don the simple white garment of baptism, was the symbol of Christianity's spiritual triumph. The Gospel of Jesus Christ had finally turned the ancient world upside down.

## THE IMPERIAL STATE CHURCH

THE Christianity of the Constantinian emperors gradually became the State Religion of the last days of the Roman empire. Imperial legislation increasingly favored the Christian Church, while at the same time the government made the lot of the pagan more difficult. Around 375 A.D., in the reign of the zealous Emperor Gratian, measures were taken to withdraw all State support from pagan religious institutions, as well as to sever the lingering connection between paganism and the ceremonies of Roman civic life. Twenty years later the Christian victory was decisive. In the year 391 paganism was proscribed by an edict of Theodosius I.

The establishment of Christianity sharply affected the social life of the empire. Christian standards were soon reflected in the new imperial social legislation. The laws of the Constantinian emperors were framed in accordance with Christian ethical ideals. At the same time the state recognized the competence of the Church's growing canon law, not only in spiritual things, but also in the other areas of life where Christian moral principles were involved. The story of this relation between Church and State, and the conflicts that ultimately sprang from it, rightly belongs to the next chapter of Church history. Here be it noted that the passionate struggle between pope and emperor that marked all medieval history had its origin in the State Church of the final years of the Roman Empire.

The victory of the faith brought a tremendous challenge to the moral and spiritual resources of the Christian Fellowship. Christianity was called to become the redemptive power in the life of a whole empire. Moreover, the challenge came precisely when the moral and spiritual strength of ancient Rome was spent. The sands of the pagan Graeco-Rome culture had finally run out. The barbarian Germanic hordes already had broken over the imperial frontiers. The task before the victorious Church in this chaotic and disintegrating order was no less than the building of a new and Christian civilization in the West. The greatest testimony to the unconquerable power of the Christian faith was the accomplishment of this task in the formation of the Medieval Commonwealth.

# CHAPTER TWO

# The Medieval Commonwealth

THE story of the thousand years between the fifth and the fifteenth centuries is the record of the rise and decline of the Medieval Commonwealth of Europe. The heroic achievements of the Church in the Dark Ages were the conversion of the barbarians and the moulding of the whole West to Christian ideals of man's common life. On the foundations of the vanished Roman Empire Christianity built a new civilized social and political order, a Christian "one-world" where the unity of men in the Body of Christ was expressed on its spiritual side in the universal Church, and in its temporal aspect in the medieval empire.

There is much to be said later concerning the corruptions of institutions and the decay in moral and spiritual strength that marked the Medieval Commonwealth in the last years of its existence. On the eve of the Reformation, Christian society in all its aspects had declined far from the ideals realized in the high Middle Ages. But in the days of its greatness, no age has produced a higher sense of duty and readier willingness to self-sacrifice, or a finer conception of man's common brotherhood in a single Christian world order. In these things, at least, medieval Europe still speaks to us across the years which separate us from the generations of men seven centuries ago.

## THE COLLAPSE OF THE ROMAN EMPIRE

THE collapse of the western half of the Roman Empire is sometimes ascribed to the hammer blows of the invading Germanic barbarians who occupied the plains of Gaul, Italy, and Spain in the fifth and sixth centuries. That view needs some qualification. The seeds of decay had long since taken firm root in the moral and spiritual fibre of Roman society. The coming of the barbarians provided the means rather than the cause of the disintegration of the old order in the West. Rome did not fall under the onslaughts of invaders; instead, the empty shell of the imperial structure was forcibly appropriated by the vigorous tribesmen from beyond the Rhine-Danube line.

Nor is invasion, with its suggestion of sudden catastrophe, quite the exact description. The barbarians came slowly at first, drifting across the borders in increasing numbers, settling in the frontier provinces in a pattern more accurately described as infiltration. Often welcomed as sturdy additions to the Romanized provincial populations, they were drawn into the life of the empire in numerous ways. Perhaps most significant, in the light of later events, was the practice of recruiting soldiers for the imperial army from among their ranks.

The peaceful assimilation of barbarian peoples depended upon the vitality of the Roman provinces. By the end of the fourth century, however, it was clear that the imperial social and political structure was no longer stable enough to control the migrating folk or to absorb them peacefully. Violent clashes took place in all the frontier provinces as the newcomers sought to rule their former masters. Breaking loose from temporary settlements, bands of tribesmen overran the West, plundering and devastating the settlements, their leaders constantly seeking a greater share of power in what remained of the imperial government. Behind them, fresh hordes poured over the borders, pushed westwards by the restless movements of Slavic tribes deep in eastern Europe.

This phase of the barbarian penetration was accompanied by violence and destruction, giving the appearance of invasion. The Gothic tribes, for example, ranging through Greece and Italy, sacked the city of Rome in the year 410, and finally settled in Italy, southern Gaul, and Spain. The Burgundians entered the Rhone valley; the Vandals, leaving a wake of terror behind them in their rapid sweep through Gaul and Spain, crossed to North Africa where they ravaged that ancient province from Gibraltar to Carthage. In the north, the heathen Anglo-Saxons descended upon Britain, while the Frankish people, destined for a greater role in European affairs than any other barbarians, settled in Gaul and western Germany.

Amid the turmoil that accompanied these rapid movements, the central imperial government disappeared, its power appropriated by the unstable barbarian kingdoms that sprang up in the former Roman provinces. Yet the political legacy of ancient Rome was strong. As the barbarians assimilated elements of western culture, they came into the inheritance of the Roman tradition of law and government. The sense of man's political unity, bequeathed to them by the empire and reinforced by the Christian doctrine of human brotherhood, found expression in the idea that their petty kings ruled as deputies of the emperor —now, of course, a shadowy figure in distant Constantinople. However nominal, this acknowledgment of the imperial principle played an important part in the fashioning of medieval Europe. The single imperial commonwealth would again come into being as a civilized and Christian order was slowly built during the Dark Ages.

## CHRISTIAN LEADERSHIP IN A CHANGING WORLD

In a time of crisis and change few men can discern the shape of things to come. Such is the experience in the uncertainties of the mid-twentieth century; it was so also in the end of the Roman Empire. Thousands sought relief from the unbearable tensions of anxiety and despair in the decadence and cynicism that characterized society in a dying world. Only among Christians was faith unshaken and hope secure. One of the remarkable features of these closing centuries of antiquity was the intellectual, evangelistic, and administrative activity of the bishops and leaders of the Church. Even as the familar political and social fabric crumbled under the barbarians, the great theological councils framed the ringing affirmations of the Christian doctrine of God and His everlasting redemptive outreach to men. Here was the assertion of ultimate meaning in life despite catastrophe, and meaning that was found in God's unchanging purpose to build the community of His people in the world of His creation.

The principles upon which the new Europe rested were bequeathed to the architects of the Medieval Commonwealth by these Christian leaders of the fourth and fifth centuries. Let us glance at the work of two of the many men whose achievements in thought and action formed a bridge over which the ancient world passed into the Middle Ages.

In 374 A.D., Ambrose of Milan, vigorous and skillful governor of the city that had become the center of Roman rule in the West, was chosen bishop by unexpected popular acclamation. Devoting himself to his new office with the same integrity and sense of duty which had marked his civil career, Ambrose's episcopate clearly reveals the prestige and authority that by this time clothed the person of the Christian bishop. Though the growing power and independence of the Church in Ambrose's day was buttressed by the imperial legislation, it was the work of such men as he that made the Christian organization the only stable institution in the changing scene.

St. Ambrose's accomplishments are too numerous to record in detail. His passionate opposition to heathen practices stimulated the imperial proscription of organized paganism in the year 391. His stubborn resistance to the Arianism of the court circles in Milan successfully checked the threatened advance of that heresy in northern Italy. But his chief importance lies in his memorable conflict with Theodosius I, the last strong emperor in the West. In this struggle Ambrose set forth those principles of the relation of Church and State that were to be central in medieval thought.

In 390 A.D. Theodosius dispatched a company of troops to restore order in the city of Thessalonica, where the governor had been murdered in a riot of the citizens. Summoning the populace to the hippodrome, the soldiers slaughtered seven thousand of them in cold blood, a crime that horrified the whole Mediterranean world, pagan and Christian alike. Ambrose acted with fearless courage. Face to face with the emperor at the door of the basilica in Milan, he barred Theodosius from the fellowship of the Church and participation in its sacramental life. Church and State stood embattled at that moment. Was the emperor above the law? Outside the reach of the code of which he was the guardian? Or was he under the Christian obligations on all men, high and low? The answer was given when Theodosius turned away from the basilica and accepted the discipline laid upon him for his sin.

Ambrose thought of Church and State as two allied but independent powers, one functioning in the spiritual sphere, the other in temporal affairs. In respect to religion, the duty of the Christian state or emperor was to protect and support the Church, enforcing the decisions of its ecumenical councils, and framing a legislative code in accordance with Christian moral principles. Beyond this the activity of the state ceased. The independence of the Church in respect to its property and its law, as well as the privileges and powers of its clergy, must be respected and guaranteed. Here, briefly, is the pattern of thought that determined the relation of Church and State in the early years of the Middle Ages, before the doctrine of the supreme and universal power of the papacy became dominant in the West. It was in sharp distinction to the principle accepted in the eastern half of the old empire. There the concept of the divinely given powers of the sacred emperor, extending to control of Church and State alike, was already widespread. The rift between the Greek East and the Roman West was further widened by these opposing views of the relation between the Christian spiritual and temporal powers.

The ideas of St. Ambrose were conveyed to succeeding generations with greater force because they were developed by a still more eminent Christian scholar and bishop, St. Augustine of Hippo. On Easter Even in 387 Ambrose baptized Augustine in Milan, and the man whose thought was to dominate Western Christendom for centuries embarked upon his career as a philosopher and theologian.

## ST. AUGUSTINE AND THE CITY OF GOD

IT IS difficult to do justice to St. Augustine and his enormous influence in shaping the traditions of Latin Christianity. The son of a devout Christian mother, St. Monica, and a pagan father, he has left a glimpse of his passionate nature and his tempestuous early life in the famous *Confessions*. There, also, he has set down the story of his conversion to Christianity, an event which is reminiscent of the spiritual crisis in the life of St. Paul. Augustine had explored the intellectual and religious resources of paganism and found them wanting. In Milan, under the influence of St. Ambrose, he discovered in the companionship of the Living Christ the ultimate reality that gives meaning to all things.

In 388 A.D. Augustine returned to his native North Africa, being chosen Bishop of Hippo a few years later. Surrounded by a small community of scholars and clergy living under a strict rule of life, he remained there until his death in the year 430. He died in the midst of the confusion accompanying the reduction of the civilization of North Africa to a ruinous state by the invading Vandals.

Augustine's episcopate was a stormy one. He was in constant conflict with the Donatists, who had separated themselve from the Church over the question of extending mercy to the apostates after the last persecution of Christianity. Donatist and Catholic churches stood side by side throughout the province; bitterness and violent conflict divided them. He was the equally firm opponent of the *Pelagians,* a new group of heretics who believed that man's salvation rested essentially upon his own efforts in goodness, rather than upon the grace given him of God.[1]

The Donatist schism and the Pelagian heresy posed to Christian theology serious questions concerning the nature of the Church and the necessity of the sacraments in the lives of Christians. These Augustine sought to answer, and many of the doctrines that he framed became central in Latin Christianity.

Against the contentions of the Donatist body, Augustine asserted the claim of the Catholic Church to be the true Church of Christ. The true Body of Christ is universal, knowing no limits of race or color, no barriers of nation, class, or culture. Inspired by the Holy Spirit, this

---

[1] *Pelagianism* is discussed at greater length in Chapter Three in connection with its appearance in English Christianity.

Body is that of man's highest membership, a fellowship of charity and love. The intolerance of the schismatic who has separated himself from that kind of fellowship, together with his sectionalism, betray the fact that he has cut himself off from the Catholic and Apostolic Church.

Within the Catholic Church alone grace is found for man's salvation. Imparted through the sacraments, it brings to man that without which he cannot be saved: the help of God. Augustine would not deny that in one sense Donatist orders and sacraments were technically valid, but the strength of his argument lay in its moral, rather than disciplinary emphasis. The sacramental character can develop and flower only within the Christian fellowship of faith and love; that is, only within the Catholic Church where that fellowship exists.

Notable as these contributions to Christian thought were, even more important was Augustine's interpretation of the meaning of history in his *City of God*. Provoked by the pagan challenge that the collapse of the Roman Empire was due to the victory of Christianity, the treatise went beyond the mere refutation of that charge to interpret the whole course of human events from the Christian point of view.

In *De civitate dei* Augustine recognizes two kinds of human community: *the commonwealth of God,* an eternal spiritual community of those whose lives are centered in the things of God; and *the commonwealth of man,* a transitory, earthly community where men seek power and prosperity, intent upon creaturely satisfactions and earthly securities. History is that process, under the providence of

God and through His redeeming grace, in which men are brought from the transitory Earthly City of this world into the abiding community of the Heavenly City of both worlds. Thus human history is not an unending series of cycles of rise, growth, and decline, but rather a continuous process in which the City of God is constantly set before men, leading them to find eternal life in its values and through its God-centered fellowship.

This contrast between Zion and Babylon, the heavenly and the earthly communities, made a powerful appeal to the imagination of people in the early Middle Ages. It is easy to see why they identified the City of God with the Church as they saw it in their own time, and why they readily consented to those papal claims which placed the Church above all kingdoms and empires of the earthly city. Today the medieval conflicts between popes and emperors are archaic and long-forgotten, but the contrast of the two cities is still present in modern form. The compelling message of the *City of God,* for any age of man, is the proclamation of the autonomy of the spiritual life. A man should be both a Christian and a good citizen, but to belong to the community of God involves him in the duties and responsibilities of a freedom that no earthly city can provide, and over which it has no final control.

### THE CHURCH AND THE BARBARIANS

THE majority of the Germanic peoples who flooded the empire in the fourth and fifth centuries had been converted to Christianity during their earlier settlement in the frontier provinces. The Goths, for example, were evangelized in great numbers through the preaching of

Ulfilas, who went out from Constantinople to work among them about 340 A.D. While the hardships endured by this missionary and his companions are part of a heroic saga now lost to history, success crowned their efforts. Ulfilas translated the Scriptures into Gothic, beginning a task which Christian missionaries have continued down to the present—that is, reducing spoken dialects to writing in order to make the Word of God available to primitive peoples.

What was true of the Goths was true to a lesser degree of the Vandals and Burgundians. Christianity had taken firm root among them. Once they had penetrated the central areas of the empire where Christian influence was dominant, their conversion was rapidly completed.

The attitude of the Germanic peoples toward the Church was, despite their violence, one of unquestioning acceptance and respect. However thin the veneer of their Christianity, they acknowledged the authority of the Church, ready to accept the principle of the autonomy of the ecclesiastical institution that had been proclaimed in the teaching of Ambrose, Augustine, and others. This attitude combined with a number of circumstances to enhance the authority and prestige of the Roman papacy during these centuries of change.

The papacy had emerged from the years of its increasing influence in the Early Church with an undefined primacy throughout the western provinces. When Constantine and his successors moved the imperial capital from Rome to Constantinople, finally leaving only a deputy to represent them in the West, much of the ancient traditional prestige that surrounded the emperor was inherited by the pope who assumed the government of the Eternal City. Furthermore, as the barbarians came into possession of the legal traditions of the empire, they accepted the wide, though loosely defined powers with which the decrees of the last emperors had clothed the papacy. Men looked toward Rome and saw there the principles of unity and stability, so long embodied in the Caesar, now expressed in the Vicar of Christ. The Christian institution alone made claims upon the allegiance of every man, symbolizing the ideal of a single European society that survived the empire which had once actualized it. The historical circumstances of these years when Europe stood upon the threshold of the Middle Ages provided the papacy with its first long step toward the supremacy later exercised by the popes.

There was, however, one vital issue that placed the barbarian Christians and the papacy in sharp conflict. Most of the new peoples were Arian Christians.[2] Converted by missionaries from the East when Arianism was enjoying its brief success in that area, the Germanic folk brought this heresy with them as they overran western Europe. Perhaps the most significant turning-point in these years, therefore, was the conversion of the heathen Franks of northern France and the lower Rhineland, not to Arianism, but to Catholic Christianity.

The vigorous and able King Clovis of the Franks was baptized in 496 A.D., an event with immense consequences for the future Commonwealth of Europe. He sprang at once into the position of the consecrated champion of Catholic orthodoxy against the Arian Germanic peoples.

[2] *Arianism* has been described in Chapter One in connection with the theological councils of the fourth and fifth centuries.

Recognized by the emperor in distant Constantinople as an allied "Consul and Augustus," hailed by the pope as "a helmet of salvation for the Church," Clovis embarked upon his speedy conquest of the Goths and other barbarians. Within a few decades the power of the Frankish Kingdom had spread over the old provinces of Gaul and the Rhineland, moulding the divided peoples into a new political unity.

The alliance between the popes and the Frankish monarchs was firmly maintained. Three centuries later, on Christmas Day in the year 800, it culminated in the coronation of Charlemagne by Pope Leo III in St. Peter's at Rome. On that day the Holy Roman Empire of the West was born.

THE MONKS AND THE DARK AGES

THE name of *The Dark Ages* is often given to the first five hundred years of the medieval period. Although it is possible to exaggerate the darkness of these centuries of transition from antiquity to the medieval world, it is still true that in a rude and barbarous age the flame of civilization was kept alive only with difficulty and by groups of men of intense Christian devotion. In this task the monastic institution of Christianity played a decisive part in moulding the West to civilized ideals.

Christian monasticism had its beginnings in the middle of the third century when the example of St. Anthony led thousands of Christian hermits into the lonely deserts of Egypt to find communion with God in a life of solitude and ascetic discipline. In these early years of experiment with a vocation to prayer and meditation, the first Christian monks were hermits. But gradually the ideal of a life of renunciation matured. The solitary cells of the hermits gave place to groups of men (and later, of women) living a common life of worship, discipline, and service under a Rule.

Between the days of St. Anthony and those of St. Augustine, a long line of devoted men of prayer explored monasticism to find its full and mature expression. Pachomius first brought the Egyptian solitaries together into community life; Basil of Caesarea extended and developed the community principal in the eastern half of the Church, providing an ideal of life that has remained central in the monasticism of the Orthodox Church down to the present day. St. Jerome, St. Martin of Tours, John Cassian, and others introduced the monastic life into the Latin West.

Monasticism had its origin partly in a protest against the growing worldliness of the Church. During the years of peace between the last two persecutions, the influx of thousands of half-converted folk inevitably brought about a compromise of Christian standards with those of the world, and a less intense self-consecration among individuals. This situation was greatly intensified when the Church made itself "at home" in the empire after its recognition by Constantine. The devotion of the monk was aroused in protest when only with difficulty a respectable Christian could be distinguished from a respectable pagan. Furthermore, this protest was directed against the ecclesiasticism that invaded the Church as the clerical order became involved with secular concerns in the imperial State Church. For many years monks were normally lay men.

anti-clerical in their outlook, suffering under the suspicion and hostility of the clergy.

If, however, historical circumstances shed light upon the rise of monasticism, they do not totally explain its nature. In the life of self-renunciation, dedicated wholly to the glory of God, and in the consequent outreach toward mankind which the vision of God inspires, there is a witness to Christian absolutes that must always be a part of Christianity. The community of those whose lives have been devoted to the things of God is a constant reminder that the Christian life on every level should be a life of corporate brotherhood, self-sacrifice, and service.

It was the power of this ideal that animated the early monastic groups in the West, like those of St. Martin of Tours in France, and made them focal points for the conversion of the barbarians and the maintenance of the virtues of civilized man. All through Europe in these dark days, little bands of monks, from the Celtic communities in the wilds of Ireland and Scotland to the Roman monasteries on the shores of the Mediterranean, slowly, but surely spread those Christian principles on which medieval society was to rest.

The man who holds highest place in the annals of western monasticism is St. Benedict of Nursia, author of the *Benedictine Rule,* whose monastery at Monte Cassino set the pattern for the common life of European monks for centuries. Benedict's historical importance lies in his naturalization of monasticism in the West. He gave it an expression that made *The Religious Life* (as it came to be called) an essential element in Latin Christianity. At the same time, he adjusted it harmoniously with the institutional life of the Church. His famous Rule was a model of moderation and discretion, setting a healthy balance between work and rest, prayer and study. Temperate in its emphasis upon ascetic discipline, the Rule places the spiritual welfare and work of each member of the monastic community above all lesser things.

Already the basic vows of the cloistered life are becoming fixed in the familiar pledges of poverty, chastity, and obedience. Underneath these lay the desire of the monk to learn to depend upon God alone, breaking human ties, and renouncing trust in earthly securities. To these disciplines St. Benedict added the rule of stability, that is, the monk should remain in the community where he first sought to fulfil his vocation. Benedict did not intend his monks to become wanderers and beggars, nor even bishops, popes, and ecclesiastical statesmen. As the years passed, however, they became all these, sometimes to the advantage of the Medieval Church, sometimes to its discredit, but never to the advancement of the true witness of the monastic community in the world.

Central in the Benedictine ideal was the regular offering of the prayer and praise of the community, the *Opus Dei*. "Seven times a day do I praise thee" was the passage of the *Psalms* which inspired the Divine Offices. Day after day, year in and year out, century upon century, men offered their corporate sacrifices of praise and thanksgiving. The harsh discords of strife and confusion that echoed through the first centuries of the medieval period gradually faded before the notes of the real theme-music of the Middle Ages—the bells of the cloisters and the chanting of the monks to the glory of Almighty God.

## ROME AND CONSTANTINOPLE

Two great patriarchates of the Early Church survived the shattering effects of the changes in the fifth and sixth centuries. They were Rome and Constantinople, centers of ecclesiastical power in the West and East respectively. But the gulf that divided Latin and Greek Christianity before the days of Constantine was still further widened by the events of the Dark Ages. In these years the cultural, political, and theological differences that were to sunder Roman Catholicism and Eastern Orthodoxy permanently in 1054 were greatly intensified.

With the rise of the Frankish Kingdom to a dominating position in Europe, what remained of the eastern half of the old empire continued to be governed by an emperor at Constantinople or, as it came to be called, Byzantium. Eastern in its tradition, and increasingly Greek in character, the Byzantine Empire gradually ceased to look westwards, being occupied almost exclusively with the problem of controlling the ancient imperial provinces of the Near East. Nor was this a simple matter. Syria and Egypt, affected by nascent nationalist movements, stirred restlessly under the political rule of a Greek government and the ecclesiastical domination of the Greek Church. Byzantium had little chance to regret the loss of the West, and less opportunity to attempt its recovery.

By the end of the seventh century the provincial nationalist problem was solved for the Greek government by the loss of territory to the rising power of the Mohammedans. The extraordinary genius of Mohammed had fused the tribes of Arabia in a militant, nationalist religion, and within a short time of his death, the followers of the prophet had defeated the Persians, overrun Syria and Asia Minor, and were entering Egypt and the North African coasts. The western conquests of Islam stretched from the Black Sea around the southern shores of the Mediterranean into the Spanish peninsula. One arm of the crescent lodged in the Pyrenees while the other pointed its threat at the gates of Constantinople. In these circumstances the Byzantine Empire was occupied almost entirely with the problem of survival. The striking achievement of the Greek emperors was their success in defending the easternmost gate of Europe for seven centuries. Constantinople did not fall to the Mohammedan Turks until 1453.

In this political scene, the West went its own way. The Frankish Kingdom became the heart of the Holy Roman Empire in 800 A.D. when Charlemagne, the ablest Christian prince of the early Middle Ages, was crowned as emperor by the pope. Byzantium was a remote fabulous city to the Westerner. The wonders and wealth of the Greek capital that travelers described belonged to another world, far from European life.

If these political and cultural differences contributed to the separation of East and West, they were further intensified by the constant ecclesiastical quarrels between the Roman popes and the Byzantine patriarchs. Such conflicts had their origin both in the pretensions of the papacy to supremacy over all Christendom, and in the theological temper dividing the philosophic and speculative Greek mind from the dogmatic and legalistic Roman religious outlook.

Furthermore, as has been indicated earlier, the position of pope and patriarch in respect to civil authority was entirely at variance. The independence of the Church from all state control was a firm principle of Latin Christianity, shortly to be expanded into the claim of papal supremacy in temporal as well as spiritual affairs. Eastern Orthodoxy, however, accepted the theory that the emperor had powers and functions which were both ecclesiastical and civil; a principle often known as *Caesaropapism*.[3] The patriarchs at Constantinople were the ecclesiastical associates of a sacred ruler who was thought to represent the divine power upon earth. Church and State were indistinguishable in the Eastern Empire. Byzantium was a Christian monarchy, ruled in all matters by an apostolic emperor.

Against this background, the ecclesiastical quarrels between Rome and Constantinople led to a series of schisms in the ninth and tenth centuries, culminating in a separation in 1054 which became permanent. The anathemas launched by pope and patriarch in that year sprang from relatively trivial disputes. The real causes of the break in Christian unity are found in the factors outlined here.

A word should be added concerning the achievements of Eastern Orthodoxy in the Middle Ages. Perhaps the most notable of these was the conversion of the Slavs, including the great mass of peoples in Russia. Nor is it without significance that throughout the centuries the Eastern Church maintained a principle of Christian unity in faith and order that did not rest upon the autocratic power of a papal institution. The Catholicism of the East

---

[3] The Caesar, or temporal monarch, has the powers of a pope, or spiritual ruler. Spiritual and temporal powers are thus conjoined in the Christian Prince. It was the exact opposite of the later papal theory that these powers were entrusted to the Vicar of Christ.

is freer and richer in character than that to which the domination of Roman Christianity accustomed the Western mind.

## THE ACHIEVEMENTS OF THE PAPACY

THE erection of a Christian civilization in barbarian Europe was the result of the combination of many forces. Intellectual and theological activity gave one kind of leadership; the ideals and devotion of the monks provided another. The sacrificial labors of missionaries built enduring foundations in faith; even the political ambitions of princes moved the West along the path toward a single Medieval Commonwealth. The coördinating spiritual principle underneath this activity was the vigorous and constructive genius of Latin Christianity. Moreover, it was a spiritual principle effectively embodied in an authoritative institution that could inspire, direct, and control all the forces at work in the new Europe. This institution was the Roman papacy.

In the turbulent centuries of the early Middle Ages perhaps only the papacy that Latin Christianity produced could have accomplished the task set before the Christian Church. Few can doubt that the papacy of this period was an instrument to God's plan and purpose in His world. Whatever the condition of the papal institution in a later age, in the first years of medieval history its achievements were remarkable.

Three things were required of an institution that assumed the leading role in building a Christian civilization in Europe. In a wider sense, the formation of Christian community in any age depends upon these same qualities.

They will not necessarily take the same forms of expression that they assumed a thousand years ago, but there is a continuing urgency upon the Church to find and bear witness to them.

The first is *a controlling sense of Christian stewardship* over both power and possessions. By this alone can the primary ecclesiastical responsibility be met—that of devoting all things to the service of God. This sense of stewardship the papacy at its best brought to the pastoral ideals of Catholicism. Secondly, there must be provided *an effective moral power* in the lives of men. This power was externalized by the medieval papacy in the development of a universal Church, or Canon Law. Finally, *the independence of the spiritual life* must be maintained against those secular forces tending to subordinate the things of God to those of Caesar. This was the mainspring of the continuous papal conflict with the temporal powers of Europe.

In the days of its greatness the papacy bore striking witness to these foundations upon which any abiding Christian community must rest. When we examine the decline of the papal Church in the end of the Middle Ages, the political and ecclesiastical struggles of the eve of the Reformation should not be allowed to divert attention from the main issue. The corruption of these ideals, and the twisting of them to the service of the papal institution instead of all Christendom, constituted the real evil in the later medieval papacy.

## FROM GREGORY I TO GREGORY VII

In the early Middle Ages the points we have been discussing are illustrated in the work of three great popes, each

71

one of whom is an architect of the Medieval Common-wealth: Gregory I, Nicholas I, and Gregory VII.

Never were the ideals of Christian stewardship set forth more compellingly than by Gregory I, pope during the years 590 to 604. Called to the papal office when the fortunes of the Church were at low ebb, and when the sudden irruption of Lombard barbarians into northern Italy threatened the very existence of the papacy, Gregory's task was a difficult one. Even he was discouraged. In one famous passage he describes the Church as "an old and violently-shattered ship, its timbers rotten, and fast becoming a wreck." Nevertheless, it was under Gregory's leadership that the unquenchable vitality of Christianity was again displayed.

By patient and astute diplomacy, Gregory I skillfully postponed the Lombard threat, making it possible for his successors to forge the alliance that would allow the Franks, as champions of the Church, to destroy the Lombard power. His careful administration of the growing territories of the Church laid a firm foundation for the temporal Papal States in central Italy. His skill in extending and organizing the institutional life of the Church in western Europe was matched only by his passionate desire to see the conversion of all the barbarians. Few men have had the missionary zeal of Gregory the Great.[4]

The significant thing, however, about Gregory's activity is its motivation. Underneath all was a deep concern for the welfare of Christendom. If he added to the power of the popes, it was not in self-interest, but rather to serve better the cause of Christ in the world in which he lived.

---

[4] The famous mission to England is discussed at length in Chapter Three.

Out of Gregory's work came a tradition of stewardship and service that set an ideal for the papacy in the centuries that followed. Nowhere is this better seen than in his treatise on the pastoral office of the Christian ministry, the *Liber Regulae Pastoralis*. Here is depicted that integrity of life and purity of motive which the Christian pastor must possess. Here, too, is that ideal of true Christian pastoral care in which the cure of souls is set before the claims of the institution. "Servant of the Servants of God" is one title in the style of the Roman pontiff. It describes Gregory's conception of the true character of the papal office.

Nearly three hundred years later, the second principle, that of effective moral power in the lives of men, was externalized in the developing canon law by another pope, Nicholas I. Nicholas came to the pontificate in the year 858, during the political disintegration which came upon Europe after the collapse of the premature Frankish Empire of Charlemagne. Imperial power will rise again among the Germanic princes, built upon the growing feudal system, but for some decades a chaos resembling that of the early barbarian period engulfed northern Europe.

Vigorous and masterful, Nicholas not only governed the papal territories as a sovereign monarch, but also successfully asserted the power of the Church's law in the face of the serious moral decay which threatened European society in his time. His treatment of the princes and states of Europe was arrogant and high-handed; his control of the bishops and provinces of the Church was an example of unprecedented papal autocracy. Nicholas was the first pope to weave into a single coherent theory of absolute power the various strands of authority that over the centuries had gradually come to be associated with the papal office.

Eventually the principles of Nicholas I became part of the later papal pretensions to a kind of power that inevitably corrupts and destroys the integrity of an institution which claims it. Yet in his own time Nicholas successfully vindicated those moral principles of Christianity that must underlie any abiding common life man seeks to build. Like Gregory before him, if he enhanced the power of the Roman pontiff it was in the interests of the maintenance of the law of God in human society. Thus, the canon law of the Church, formed partly from the regulations of councils and partly by papal decree, began to assert its competence in those areas of human activity where Christian moral standards were involved.

The pope who struggled hardest to preserve the autonomy of the spiritual life against the attacks of secularism was Gregory VII, two centuries after Nicholas I. The sweeping program of reform that he and his associates launched in the last years of the eleventh century was directed chiefly against the control of Church offices and appointments by the monarchs, princes, and barons of feudal Christendom.[5] The bitterest contest of medieval Europe was that between Gregory VII and the Emperor Henry IV, a struggle in which the Church fought to

---

[5] The conflicts of Church and State in feudal Europe, as well as those between canon law and king's law, are described in detail in Chapter Three where the medieval English Church is discussed. Illustrations of principles discussed in this chapter are provided in the context of the history of our own tradition.

maintain the things of God free from control by those of Caesar.

The *Investiture Controversy,* as this conflict over the appointment of higher ecclesiastics is called, was but one phase of the clash between the temporal and spiritual powers of Christendom. The Church waged an equally stubborn battle to enforce the discipline of clerical celibacy, and to eliminate the gross evil of simony—the buying and selling of church offices. The aim of the Church in the whole struggle was to gain freedom from secular interference and lay control, freedom to regulate every aspect of its own life.

The claims made by Gregory VII and his successors in the interests of this freedom sweepingly arrogated all power, temporal and spiritual alike, to a pope who was the very Vicar of Christ upon earth. He alone could make and unmake kings; he alone could be judged by no earthly tribunal. This passionate declaration of universal papal supremacy was the form in which the Medieval Church asserted its spiritual freedom, the theory whereby the Gregorian papacy sought to safeguard the principle of the independence of things spiritual. Tragedy lay in the very character of the claim itself. Within it were the seeds of that terrible corruption which absolute power always brings. But in the eleventh century, at least, these seeds had not yet produced rank decay in the integrity of the papal institution. Principle stood first in the mind of Gregory VII. Power existed primarily for the welfare of the cause of Christ over that of earthly standards and securities. The tragic consequences of a claim to absolute power lay hidden in the distant future.

IN THE opening years of the thirteenth century, greatest of all centuries of the Middle Ages, the Christian Commonwealth enjoyed its brief period of full maturity. A "one-world" had come into being in the West where the unity of all men in the Body of Christ was expressed on its spiritual side in a universal papacy, and in its temporal aspect in the medieval empire. These two were but different expressions of man's single membership in a visible theocratic commonwealth. Within that one society the *regnum* and the *sacerdotium,* that is, the temporal and spiritual powers, were rooted in a single source, the fulness of all power claimed by the Roman pontiff. Temporal authority was described as subordinate to and derivative from the ultimate spiritual dominion entrusted to the papacy.

It was this political theory on which the thirteenth-century papacy acted in its relations with the princes of Europe. The great principles that the popes from Gregory I to Gregory VII had sought to make the foundation of a Christian world order were now expressed in a papal absolutism which knew no bounds. Innocent III, for example, the most eminent statesman to hold the papal office, ruled Europe in 1215 with an iron hand. Aragon, Portugal, the Scandinavian kingdoms, and a number of other small States were direct feudal fiefs of the papacy, acknowledging its temporal suzerainty and paying an annual tribute. Philip Augustus of France was humbled by the terrible weapon of the *interdict,* under which Pope Innocent placed his kingdom in order to bring the king to obedience.[6] Across

---

[6] The interdict placed a ban upon the services of the Church and the administration of the sacraments in the area upon which the judgment was pronounced. The innocent suffered with the guilty, and the salvation of all was believed to be imperiled.

the channel, King John surrendered the crown of England to the hands of the papal representative, receiving it back as Innocent's feudal vassal, promising tribute and binding his "successors and heirs forever" to recognize the temporal overlordship of the papacy.

The supremacy of the Church at the zenith of its power was displayed in the sessions of the Fourth Lateran Council of 1215. The vast assemblage of bishops and other representatives summoned by Innocent III approved canons aimed at centralizing the government of the Church, checking the spread of heresy, and imposing a strict doctrinal uniformity everywhere in Europe. The effect of these regulations was to make papal control doubly effective.

Yet already the signs of moral and spiritual decay had appeared, perhaps most clearly in the story of the Crusades. In the eleventh century a series of attempts to wrest the Holy Land from Moslem rule was launched and encouraged by the papacy. The chivalry of Europe embarked with enthusiasm upon this holy war, and in 1099 Jerusalem was taken. For nearly two centuries the Christian forces struggled to maintain the footholds secured along the coasts of Palestine. During these years the motivation of the crusading expeditions changed. Men were moved less by zeal to recover the holy places from the infidel, and more by political and economic considerations. Jealousy and personal ambition divided the kings and barons of the Christian armies. Because problems of supply made them dependent upon the fleets of the Italian mercantile cities, the economic interests of Venice and other commercial centers became a controlling factor in the later Crusades.

Only a few years before the Fourth Lateran Council the

change in the character of the Crusades was revealed in one of the most wanton crimes of history. In 1204 the expedition known as the Fourth Crusade turned aside from its goal, to capture and loot the city of Constantinople amid frightful scenes of slaughter and destruction. The protestations of Pope Innocent went unheeded by men in the grip of a lust for wealth and power.

The implications of these changing undercurrents were not perceived in the century of the Church's supremacy. Even the long and bitter conflict between the successors of Innocent III and the empire of Frederick II was seen only as a repetition of the familiar rivalry of pope and emperor in medieval Christendom. Actually, it was much more than that. The political ambitions of Frederick and the other Hohenstaufen emperors threatened the very existence of the Church's temporal authority. In the last years of the thirteenth century the secular state was in process of formation, and sensing a danger it could not wholly identify, the papacy made a stupendous effort to destroy Frederick's empire.

Victory went to the Church, but it proved to be a disastrous triumph. The defeat of the medieval empire shattered the old imperial concept of Europe's unity that had endured so many centuries, and forecast the end of the universal papal supremacy which had been so closely associated with it. At the end of the conflict the exhausted papacy could no longer maintain the Church's supremacy.

## THE HIGH MIDDLE AGES

BEFORE describing the collapse of the papacy, a word should be said about some of the characteristic aspects of medieval Christian life. Though much of the history of this period is necessarily devoted to the rise and decline of the papal monarchy, there are other phases of Christian activity that must be recorded.

Perhaps the most striking contrast with today is the real and effective human community that everywhere marked the high Middle Ages. The primary citizenship of men was in an earthly Christian Commonwealth, itself but the temporal aspect of their enduring membership in a Church that linked heaven and earth. This sense of Christian brotherhood was strong on every level of medieval life. The feudal system, for example, with its regulated privileges and responsibilities gave expression to it on the political and economic side. The guild organizations that dominated the world of crafts and commerce underlined men's essential community in labor. But at its highest this principle was proclaimed and empowered in the common worship of a Church that was inseparable from every activity of medieval life.

The very real synthesis of all human activity toward which medieval society pointed was the result of a remarkable effort to relate all things to Almighty God. In this sense, at least, the Middle Ages were "ages of faith." Glaring and shocking contrasts there were—between the ideals of chivalry, for example, and the unbridled behavior of the knights; or between the rude luxury of the barons and the abject poverty of the peasant serfs. But medieval man lived so close to the horizons of eternity that the inequities of this world were often less important than the justice that all would receive in the next.

The aspiring faith of medieval folk is expressed in the

lofty spires of the Gothic cathedrals and churches that still dominate the European cities and countryside. From Scotland to the Mediterranean the finest monuments of the Medieval Commonwealth are the exquisite pinnacles of stone which point to the things eternal, reminders that the ultimate meaning of human life lies outside the City of Man. If architecture reflects the orientation of the society that produces it, something of the real atmosphere of the Middle Ages surrounds us when we stand in a medieval church.

The rich decoration of the altar, the gleaming candles and rising incense of the chancel, the music of the choir, all impress the senses with the fulfilment of life in the Church Triumphant. Heaven is still veiled from men in this life; the tracery of the rood screen hides from men's eyes the full beauty within. All around us are the sculptured and painted figures of the saints, standing among the memorials of those who have gone before into the Church Expectant. Above stretch the battlements of the City of God, the soaring tower rising out of them capped with a slender beckoning finger of stone. Even today the most casual visitor may still catch a fleeting glimpse of the spirituality of men and women eight hundred years ago.

The synthesis underlying so much of medieval life was reflected also in the intellectual activity of Christian theologians and philosophers in the Middle Ages. Revivals of learning accompanied each period of the Church's reinvigoration, beginning in the days of Charlemagne and leading to the finest achievements of scholasticism in the thirteenth century.

The scholastic philosophers of the Medieval Church

were men who sought to join faith with reason, religion and knowledge in a single coherent system of thought. They came into a twofold intellectual heritage. On one hand was a body of truth known only through God's revelation, the dogmas of Catholicism that had been formulated in the Early Church. On the other were those truths that men had discovered by the use of human reason, an inheritance largely from the Platonic and Aristotelian philosophy of antiquity. The problem that occupied the minds of the great medieval thinkers was that of constructing a synthesis of these two, welding revelation and reason together in a single ordered system embracing all reality.

There was considerable diversity among early medieval theologians. St. Anselm, for example, based his profound religious insights upon the axiom *credo ut intelligam* (I believe in order that I may understand). Acceptance of truth by faith was the first step in knowledge. For Anselm the philosophy of religion rested upon religious experience and was tested by it. Peter Abelard, however, would reverse the Anselmic phrase: *Intelligo ut credam* ( I understand in order that I may believe). Refusing to rest his faith upon authority uncritically accepted, Abelard was the champion of rationalism. He scandalized the men of his times, but in many ways his methods prepared the way for the greater scholastics who followed.

The most eminent of medieval schoolmen was the Dominican friar, St. Thomas Aquinas. His *Summa Theologica* was the most notable intellectual feat of the Middle Ages. In it he systematized the whole range of Christian doctrinal and philosophic thought. His influence was enormous in later centuries; his system is the official philosophy of Roman Catholicism today. Christian theologians who have swayed the thought of millions, and on whose exposition of doctrine whole traditions have rested, are few— St. Paul, St. Augustine, Martin Luther, John Calvin—but among them St. Thomas Aquinas holds high place.

## MEDIEVAL SPIRITUALITY

THE variety of expression that characterized the piety and devotion of the Medieval Church is best illustrated by a glance at some of the spiritual leaders of the Middle Ages.

St. Bernard of Clairvaux represents all that was best in twelfth-century monasticism. Trained at Citeaux, he ultimately became abbot of the Cistercian house at Clairvaux, and the outstanding personality of his time. The monastic revival that had been launched a century before by the Reformed Benedictines of Cluny was carried to new heights of influence by St. Bernard and the Cistercians.

Sternly self-disciplined, yet joyous in his zeal, Bernard extended his spiritual power into the lives of thousands. Unhesitatingly rebuking kings, popes, and bishops, consulted on every cause in Europe, he was a moral reformer, a missionary, an evangelistic preacher, and a staunch defender of the faith all at the same time. His abiding contribution was made to Christian mysticism. St. Bernard was a mystic, a man who sought God through his affections. *Jesus, the very thought of thee with sweetness fills the breast*—the lines of this familiar twelfth-century hymn, if not by Bernard himself, express perfectly the spirit of his devotion. St. Bernard's mysticism was surrounded by moral safeguards. He knew that the experience of the vision of God was necessary to any moral advance in the Christian life. But he knew also that the vision of God is ever tested by the loving service of mankind that it inspires.

No name in Christian spiritual history is better known than that of St. Francis of Assisi, contemporary of Innocent III and the founder of a new kind of religious order called the *Friars*. Out of the restless undercurrents of the century of the Church's supremacy came a widespread evangelical movement on the part of ordinary folk, seeking a return to the simplicities of apostolic life, longing to witness to the power of Christ in their lives. Suspect of heresy, the opposition of the hierarchy drove many of them to separate themselves from the Church. Such, for example, were the Waldensians. One stream of this movement, however, found a channel within the Church's life: the Franciscans of St. Francis and the Dominicans of St. Dominic.

Francis inspired his disciples with the ideals of poverty, humility, and complete consecration to the service of men for Jesus' sake. Instilling in them a warm and joyous devotion to their divine Companion, he drew together the little bands of friars who sought to live by the Gospel precepts. Out among the poor and the desolate of the crowded medieval towns they went, caring lovingly for the sick, the dying, and those for whom no man cared, preaching passionately the reconciling love of Christ for all men.

The spiritual power of the Franciscans speedily made them the most effective religious force in the thirteenth century. Obedient to a Rule that implemented their activities in the world, the influence of the friars was felt on every level of medieval life. Their earnest preaching and lofty pastoral ideals transformed the religion of the parishes; their missionary zeal stretched out to carry the Cross deep into Asia. Their hospitals and schools sprang up in town after town; their scholars controlled much of the intellectual life of the universities. All this was far from the simple intentions of their saintly founder, yet it revealed the vigor with which the monastic institution could adjust and transform itself to meet the religious needs of the age. Something of the spirit of St. Francis, however, lingered in the order and was manifested in periodic revivals of his original ideals. Something, too, of his unquenchable spirit passed into the heritage of spirituality that we have received from the Middle Ages.

Our rich tradition of prayer and praise owes much to medieval piety. This is readily seen in our hymnody. More than seventy-five medieval hymns are included in the Hymnal, many of them among the most familiar music of the Church's worship.[7] On Palm Sunday, for example, we are taken back to the days of Charlemagne when we sing the verses of Theodulph of Orleans: *All glory, laud, and honor: To thee, Redeemer, King!* Easter is hailed in the words of St. John of Damascus: *Come, ye faithful, raise the strain,* and in the stanzas of the fourteenth-century song: *Jesus Christ is risen today, Alleluia!* Many of the Communion hymns belong to this age of medieval spirituality. No less than five are from the pen of St. Thomas Aquinas, including the familiar lines:

> *O Saving Victim, opening wide*
> *The gate of heaven to man below,*
> *Our foes press on from every side,*
> *Thine aid supply, thy strength bestow.*

[7] *The Hymnal of the Protestant Episcopal Church* (1940).

## THE FALL OF THE MEDIEVAL PAPACY

AT THE turn of the fourteenth century came the first warning of the catastrophe that ultimately destroyed both the Medieval Commonwealth and the universal supremacy of the pope. In 1303 the papal power suffered a crushing blow at the hands of the King of France. French national self-interest, when threatened by Pope Boniface VIII, suddenly revealed itself strong enough to challenge the papal monarchy.

Boniface and Philip IV quarreled over the right of that monarch to tax the clergy and the resources of the Church within his domain in support of the war with England. The pope, invoking the canon law and acting in the tradition of Innocent III, sternly condemned Philip's procedure. But in the seventy-five years that separated Boniface VIII from the absolute power of his predecessor, the European political situation had changed. Everywhere the claims of a new national self-consciousness had gained ground. Europe stood on the threshold of modern times. Theories of royal and nationalist absolutism rose to challenge those papal and universal. Deep fissures were uncovered in the political unity of Europe, ever-widening cracks that would shortly divide the old single Commonwealth into the separate national states, and ultimately destroy the old single ecclesiastical loyalty to the papacy.

Philip IV ignored the condemnation of Boniface VIII, and when the pope arrogantly threatened France with stronger measures, the king's men seized Boniface, holding him prisoner and arousing his enemies in Italy against him. This bold action, revealing the weakness of the old theocratic claims in the face of the vigorous and growing self-concern of the nations, dealt papal prestige a blow from which it never recovered. Nor was the humiliation of Boniface VIII the end of the matter. His successor, Clement V, was induced by Philip to move the pontifical court away from the turbulence of Rome to the quiet palaces of Avignon, a tiny papal principality in southern France. There the popes remained for seventy-one years, in the famous *Babylonish Captivity* of the papacy.

In the eyes of Europe the Avignon popes, a long line of French bureaucrats, were allies of France and willing tools of the political ambitions of its king. Their commands aroused opposition; their exorbitant financial exactions were bitterly resented. This restless dissatisfaction was intensified as the papal court of Avignon became increasingly corrupt, morally and spiritually. Long before the end of the fourteenth century, men were convinced that the principles upon which the greatness of the papacy had once rested were now sacrificed to the interests of power for its own sake.

## THE PAPAL SCHISM

THE events of the papal elections of 1378 appeared to justify this conviction. Gregory XI had returned the papal court to Rome in 1376. When he died, two years later, the election fell upon the tyrannical and quarrelsome Urban VI. But shortly after he had taken office, some of the cardinals, smarting under Urban's violent treatment of them, fled from Rome and elected another pope. These cardinals longed for the luxurious ease of Avignon, as well as for the oligarchical control of the Church to which the bureaucracy there had accustomed the members of the Sacred College. Throughout Europe men viewed this scandalous schism as the moral consequence of a spiritual decay attacking the very heart and center of the Church.

The schism continued nearly forty years, despite all attempts to heal it. Half the nations of Europe acknowledged the Roman pope, the other half recognized his rival at Avignon. In this atmosphere of disunity anti-papalism flourished. Bargaining with each pope, threatening to withdraw obedience, the various governments gained more effective control over areas of national life hitherto subject to the unquestioned power of the Church. Moreover, the breakdown of a single central authority was reflected in the decline of spiritual discipline and the growth of ecclesiastical abuses that characterized the Church in the last century before the Reformation.

Cries for reform began to be raised on all sides. Questions were openly disputed concerning the very nature of the papal office. Was an absolutist papacy part of the true constitution of the Church? Was there not a deeper principle of unity in Christendom than that of allegiance to an institution which was itself divided in schism? It is not without significance that the days of the papal schism were those during which the teachings of Wycliffe spread in England, and the evangelical preaching of John Hus aroused Bohemia.

## THE UNITY OF EUROPE

THE days of the papal schism were also those of the Renaissance that ushered in the modern world. Fifteenth-century Europe was stirred by social, political, and economic changes marking the end of the Middle Ages. Everywhere the feudal system was fast disappearing. The new political life was that of the national monarchies; the emerging economic order saw the rise of the middle classes in both craft and commerce.

Underneath this restlessness were far-reaching cultural changes, destined to re-orient the whole outlook of man. Spurred on by the rediscovery of the creative genius of ancient Greece, men were absorbed in their own abilities and inflamed by their own powers. Humanism was the characteristic motif of the Renaissance. On all sides the old narrow horizons of medieval life expanded with breathless rapidity. Columbus and Magellan followed those horizons over the uncharted seas, Copernicus explored the limitless spaces amid the stars, and Leonardo da Vinci turned men's minds to that strange realm where art and science join hands.

Nearly every aspect of the Renaissance expressed itself in a struggle for emancipation from the shackles of authority. A questioning, critical spirit was unloosed upon the age-old traditions by which human activity had been governed. The Church was so deeply rooted in the former order of things that the storm of change beat heavily upon the ecclesiastical institution.[8]

In the revolutionary atmosphere of the Renaissance a daring experiment was launched by men who foresaw the destruction of the unity of Europe. Convinced that the principle of papal supremacy could no longer hold together a rapidly disintegrating order, they embarked upon

[8] Here, as earlier in this chapter, events are sketched in outline. A fuller discussion of the character of the Church on the eve of the Reformation, as well as a description of the impact of the Renaissance on religion, will be found in the following chapter.

what is called the Conciliar Movement. This was an attempt to end the papal schism and reconstitute the life of the Church by means of a General Council, that ancient representative Christian assembly which had been so prominent in the Early Church. The experiment was a bold one. The Church's law knew no council save one summoned by the pope; the tradition of papal autocracy left no room for any authoritative conciliar action. Nevertheless, taking refuge in the principle of necessity, the leaders of the movement called the three great councils of the fifteenth century.

The first was a failure—or perhaps, a rehearsal for the others. Hastily summoned at Pisa in 1409, the council declared the rival popes deposed and elected a new pontiff. But as the nations were not yet ready to make effective the conciliar decisions, the result was to aggravate the schism by adding another claimant for the papal office.

More careful planning preceded the council held at Constance in 1414-1418. Representatives came with a determination to end the schism once and for all. Success crowned the efforts of the second council. The deposition of the popes of all three lines cleared the way for the election of Martin V in 1417. The long papal schism came to an end.

The revolutionary decree of the Council of Constance was that called *Sacrosancta,* a declaration that the final authority in the Church rested not in the papacy, but in the whole body of the faithful, represented in an ecumenical council. "The Council of Constance," it ran, "declares that it has its authority immediately from Christ; and that all men, of every rank and condition, including the pope himself, are bound to obey it in matters concerning the Faith . . . and the reformation of the Church of God in its head and its members."

Here was the audacious attempt to return to the constitution of the Catholic Church centuries earlier. Papal autocracy was to be limited by vesting the highest spiritual authority in a council representative of all Christendom. The Council of Constance tried to halt the growth of papalism, returning to an ancient principle of spiritual power to which it was hoped that nations of Europe could give a common allegiance.

The Conciliar Movement was a tragic failure. Once the Council of Constance had disbanded, Martin V was free to repudiate its principles and undertake the restoration of papal control of the Church. Moreover, the new nationalism that could assert itself successfully against the power of an autocratic papacy was too strong to be checked by a theoretic conciliar principle which commended itself chiefly to academic and doctrinaire opinion. While the third General Council at Basel strove vainly to make effective reforms in the spiritual and administrative condition of the Renaissance Church, the successors of Martin V quietly recovered their supremacy through a series of concordat agreements with the monarchs of Europe.

In 1460 Pope Pius II published the bull *Execrabilis,* condemning the principle of conciliar supremacy as an outburst of rebellion against the powers rightfully belonging to the Vicar of Christ. The Conciliar Movement was over. But the path to the Reformation was laid open by the papal victory. Violent revolt was the consequence of the failure of peaceful constitutional reform.

# CHAPTER THREE

# Christianity in England

WE TURN back now to retrace our steps through the story of Christianity in England before the Reformation. *Anglicanism,* a term used to distinguish the peculiar ethos of our Church life from that of Roman Catholicism or typical Protestantism, has its roots deep in the Christian history of the English nation. Like other branches of the Anglican Communion, the Protestant Episcopal Church finds its heritage stretching back for centuries in the life of the English Church. For that reason some special knowledge of historical Anglicanism is the initial step in a better understanding of our own tradition.

Today the Churches of the Anglican Communion are marked by a catholicity which in its varied spiritual experience and in its comprehensive character claims to approximate the spirit of the ancient Church more closely than that of any other Christian body. Is this claim justified? We often confidently assert that we hold peculiar treasures in trust for all Christendom. Have we a right so to defend Anglicanism? These questions need honest answers today. They involve us in a responsibility to the rest of Christendom that demands every ounce of the spiritual courage and integrity we can muster. To answer these questions rightly we must look first at the historical tradition in which the claims of Anglicanism are rooted.

## CHRISTIANITY IN ROMAN BRITAIN

CHRISTIANITY spread to Britain in much the same way that the faith found a path to all the far corners of the empire of the Caesars. The military campaigns of nearly a century, from the exploratory landings of Julius Caesar to the successful operations of the Emperor Claudius, carved out the ancient Roman province of Britannia. Roughly speaking, that portion of the British Isles equivalent to modern England became subject to Roman rule. Here the last vestiges of organized opposition to the legionaries disappeared about the time St. Paul set out on his first missionary journey in the distant Mediterranean. For three centuries Roman Britain was destined to enjoy its place in the empire before the first Germanic raiders gave warning of the disruptive barbarian invasions.

Unlike the older provinces of Spain and Gaul, Britannia for all these years remained a frontier or soldiers' province. The eagles of the legions were never securely planted in the wild hill country of Wales nor north of the Clyde. The savage tribesmen in the west, the Picts and Scots in Ireland and Scotland—all these succeeded in making border warfare a constant factor in the administration of the province of Britain.

The conquered Britons were Celtic folk, cousins to the Celts of Roman Gaul across the channel. As one might expect, the existing contacts between the Gauls and the Britons were immensely increased when both became provincials of the Roman Empire. The narrow arm of the sea, which at times in her history served to isolate England from the rest of Europe, at other times became a connecting thoroughfare. So it was in the days of the imperial rule. Traders, travelers, soldiers, colonists, and missionaries crossed and recrossed the channel. With this traffic Christianity found its way into Britain by the year 175.

Precisely how or when the first Christian community in Britain received its start is impossible to tell. A heroic missionary story of the spread of the Gospel to this northwestern limit of the Roman Empire has been lost beyond recovery. Quite naturally, later centuries witnessed the growth of a number of legends explaining the appearance of the first Christians, the most beautiful being the charming medieval tale of Joseph of Arimathea and his companions. The famous Glastonbury thorn tree, miraculously springing from Joseph's staff, supposedly marks the spot where his company ended their long journey from the Holy Land. However fanciful the legend may be, it does bear witness to the antiquity of a Christian settlement at Glastonbury. Here in the southwestern part of England were perhaps the first witnesses to the faith of Jesus Christ. By 200 A.D. there is clear evidence of a community of Christians in Britain, as yet neither large nor strong; but nonetheless, as later events reveal, firmly rooted among the people of the Island.

## THE EARLY BRITISH CHURCH

FOR more than a hundred years there is little information about this British Church that can be transferred with confidence from the pages of legend to those of history. In fact, not until the last imperial persecution in the first years of the fourth century do events in Christian Britain emerge clearly into the light of history.

In that persecution the most famous British martyr was a provincial soldier named Alban. Sheltering a hunted priest, Alban was seized by the authorities when the hiding place of the fugitive was discovered. To the surprise of the officers, Alban confessed himself a Christian convert, and chose to pay the penalty of death rather than deny his allegiance to Jesus Christ. One of the best-loved English saints, Alban wins whole-hearted admiration for his courageous protection of the weak and the persecuted, as well as for the steadfast loyalty with which he affirmed his new-found faith. Yet the zeal of the nameless priest should not go unnoticed. In his devotion to his Lord there was a missionary outreach which won the heart of Alban in the brief time this forgotten fugitive spent under his protection.

The impression that the early Christian community in Britain was neither strong nor influential is confirmed by the events following the recognition of Christianity by the Emperor Constantine. British Churchmen attended the great councils of the fourth century. Three bishops from Britain, for example, are among the ecclesiastics whom Constantine gathers at Arles in 314 A.D. to discuss the controversies which disturb the peace of Christianity in its new-found freedom as a licensed religion.

But there is no sign of intellectual or administrative vigor in the distant provincial Church. In fact, the only Briton to capture the attention of all Christendom in these decades is a man universally denounced as a dangerous heretic: Pelagius, sometimes a British monk, now a teacher wandering around the Mediterranean, ardently proclaiming his own view of the nature of man and the way of his salvation.

The Pelagian heresy is perhaps man's primal erroneous view about himself. Like all half-truths it has been exceedingly attractive to man's pride in many generations. Despite the vigorous opposition of Augustine and other orthodox Fathers in Pelagius' own time, and despite the continued condemnation of this heresy as it appeared down through the centuries under one name or another. Indeed, it has survived into the present time.

Pelagius was impatient with the notion that man could not find salvation without the help of God's grace and strength. For him, salvation consisted in finding and living the good life. If Jesus has shown man the path he must walk, it is folly to think that God would set before man a goal which he could not attain and before which his own nature left him helpless. That there is within all men a strong pull toward sin, toward choosing the service of self instead of the service of God, Pelagius would admit. But that this tendency to the evil choice was so strong that only by the constant help of God's grace can men overcome it, seemed to Pelagius to deny the perfection of God's creation. In other words, Pelagius regarded the doctrine of original sin as immoral. It undermined the Christian sense of personal responsibility.

95

Pelagius had hold of a half-truth; that is what makes his doctrine so attractive. But, carried to its logical conclusion, it would have proclaimed a Gospel calling upon each man to save himself by his own efforts. By making man the creator of his own good character, Pelagianism appealed powerfully to man's pride. No matter in what noble terms it expressed itself at the outset, it inevitably ended in the fundamental temptation as old as the Garden of Eden that man should deny the dependent childhood which was his true relation to God.

Pelagianism in Britain at the turn of the fifth century was sufficiently widespread for the orthodox to appeal to the mother-church in Gaul for help in combating it. The last glimpses of British Christianity before the darkness of the Teutonic invasions are those of St. Germanus and other Gallic bishops conducting a vigorous preaching tour of the island, recalling British Christians to the realities of man's true nature and relation to God.

The success of the orthodox preachers was partly due to the despair attending the breakdown of the provincial civilization in Britain. Already the heathen invaders from the Germanic coasts were sailing up the rivers and estuaries, spreading destruction in raids of ever-increasing intensity. The barbarian invasions were in full flood in Europe. The Roman Empire was rapidly disintegrating. By the middle of the fifth century the raids of the Angles and the Saxons became invasions in force. Those Britons who were not massacred or enslaved fled before them, withdrawing into the security of the Welsh hills or trekking northwards into Strathclyde on the west coast of Scotland. With them went British Christianity. The darkness settled over the province as the heathen Anglo-Saxon tribes made England their new homeland.

## THE ROMAN MISSION TO ENGLAND

NORTHWESTERN Europe emerged slowly from the chaos produced by the years of barbarian penetration of the empire. For a century and a half after the collapse of the imperial structure the old path of influence and communication between England and Rome was closed. Across it lay a wide belt of Teutonic peoples who had moved westward into Gaul and the Rhineland. But by the year 596 some orderly patterns were discernible in the new Europe. In England the heathen invaders were forming the numerous petty kingdoms into which Anglo-Saxon England was divided. In Gaul the Franks had become the dominant folk among the settling tribes, and, more important, had been converted to Christianity by the heroic missionary efforts of the Church. Once more the path was open from Rome to England. Christian influence and activity could again travel the same road on which the conquering power of the Caesars once went forth from the imperial city.

The occupant of the papal office at this moment, and thus the embodiment in barbarian eyes of much of the prestige of ancient Rome, was a statesman of unusual devotion and ability. During his pontificate Gregory I, as already said,[1] set a standard for integrity of administration, devoted pastoral care, and intense missionary vigor which was unequaled by the papacy for a thousand years. Realizing that the opportunity had come for drawing the old

---

[1] See Chapter Two, pages 72-73.

British province into the new Christian Europe, he dispatched a mission to England, led by St. Augustine of Canterbury.

In the year 597 Augustine and his monks landed in Kent, the territory of the most powerful of the Anglo-Saxon petty kings, Ethelbert. Their local success was immediate. Within a short time the king and his people accepted Christianity, a Church was founded at Canterbury that was destined to become the center of the Anglican Communion, and plans had been made for missionary efforts in the other tribal States of the Angles and the Saxons. Unfortunately, everywhere outside the little Kentish kingdom progress was slow. The Gospel encountered a stubborn and deeply intrenched heathenism; Augustine's preachers met with bitter hostility.

## ROMAN AND CELTIC CHRISTIANITY

POPE Gregory was aware that remnants of the older British Christianity might be encountered by his missionaries. Among his instructions given to Augustine was the commitment of "the bishops of Britain to your care, that the ignorant may be taught, the weak strengthened, and the perverse corrected by authority." Gregory was convinced that British Christians who might be discovered by his missionaries would need to be recalled to the true faith, as well as subjected to the growing central authority of Rome in western Christendom.

To some extent the pope was justified. Bitterly hostile to the Anglo-Saxons, the Celtic British Christians had been content to maintain their religion in the isolation of the Welsh hills, making no efforts to convert the heathen invaders. Augustine discovered that attempts at negotiation with the Britons were fruitless. They looked with suspicion upon the foreign Christians who not only appeared to be on friendly terms with the hated Saxons, but who also spoke of the authority of a Roman pope about whom the Celts knew little.

But there was another branch of Celtic Christianity, concerning the extent and importance of which neither Gregory nor Augustine had much knowledge. This was the heroic missionary Church of the Irish Celts.

Before the collapse of the Roman Empire, Christianity had found its way slowly through Wales and across the narrow sea to gain a foothold in the coastal villages of Ireland. To the north in Strathclyde and Galloway Christian heroes like St. Ninian and St. Kentigern had established tiny centers of evangelization before the end of the fourth century.

It was St. Patrick, indefatigable missionary and gifted organizer, whose energy and devotion fanned these little embers of Christianity into a mighty flame that swept from Ireland over Scotland and the western isles. For over a century after his death in 461 A.D. the peculiar development of Celtic Christianity continued. Celtic monks moved restlessly from place to place, sometimes in company, sometimes in solitude, enduring incredible hardships. They were seized by a Christian vocation that was at once marked by the austerity of extreme asceticism and the enthusiasm of zealous missionary activity.

The culminating point of this development was the establishment of a Christian community at Iona in the year 563 by St. Columba. This settlement in Argyleshire on the western Scottish coast became the heart and center of the Celtic Church. For more than a hundred years the spirit of St. Columba inspired the efforts of the Celtic missionary monks, while the monastery at Iona controlled and governed the loosely organized Celtic Church of the north. St. Columba's life work was done before the Roman mission had reached England. He died in the same year Augustine landed in Kent.

## ROME OR IONA?

As AUGUSTINE'S successors gradually extended their evangelizing efforts northwards it was inevitable that they should encounter the Celtic missionaries whose travels brought them down from Scotland. The two Christian forces met in Northumbria on the northeastern coast of England. There the center of evangelization was the monastery of St. Aidan at Lindisfarne, a daughter-house of Iona. When the Roman influences appeared, King Oswy of Northumbria, though himself trained in the Celtic tradition, was well aware that unity between the two groups of Christians was essential, not only for the religious peace of his kingdom, but also for the conversion of the remaining petty states that were still overwhelmingly heathen.

The famous debate that took place at the council called by Oswy at Whitby in 664 A.D. centered upon the differing customs of the Roman and Celtic usages. We are somewhat impatient with religious quarrels over the precise date upon which the Easter festival should be observed, or the fashion in which a clergyman should trim his hair. But often in the course of history ecclesiastical controversy has avoided the main issue at stake. At Whitby the real question was one of authority and the orientation of ecclesiastical allegiance. *Should English Christianity look to Rome or Iona?*

The choice was a critical one. On one hand stood Celtic Christianity, its claim attested in the devotion and heroism of its missionaries and monks, its achievement the conversion of the north. On the other hand was the Roman Church, making its supreme and successful effort to rebuild the West into the new unity of Christian Europe. Oswy had little doubt as to the proper course. The decision was given for Rome. Northumbria would align herself, and eventually all England, with the great Church of the West.

## THE FOUNDATIONS OF THE NATIONAL CHURCH

THE decision at Whitby had far-reaching effects upon the Christian history of England. Its evangelizing force spent, Celtic Christianity tended more and more to become a backwater of customs and practices peculiar to itself. To look further toward Iona would isolate England religiously from the new forces on the continent, whereas opening the gates to the main stream of western Christianity would bring the Island within the social, political, and cultural influences of Europe. Such was the long-range result of Oswy's decision. Nonetheless, English Christianity was richer for its heritage of Celtic piety and zeal. The conquest of barbarism on the northern coasts of Europe and in the Atlantic Isles was the crowning achievement of these Celtic Christian heroes. Something of their spirit lingered in the Saxon Church.

The immediate gain was unity among Christians in England. English political unity was a gradual achievement. In fact, not for three hundred years will the petty Anglo-Saxon states finally disappear into the single kingdom. But in that long period of time the strongest force welding the divided tribes into a united nation will be the Church common to them all. The Church of England is not only older than the kingdom, but also the chief architect of its existence.

The four centuries which elapse between Whitby and the coming of William the Conqueror in 1066 are centuries of development in the Saxon Church, the formative years of the Church of England. In this period the foundations of the national English Church are laid; here many of the distinguishing marks of Anglicanism have their beginnings. A glance at the work of three men in these centuries will reveal some of the most important elements in the life of Saxon Christianity.

### ARCHBISHOP THEODORE OF CANTERBURY

THEODORE of Tarsus, a Greek scholar and philosopher of St. Paul's own city, was sent from Rome to England as Archbishop of Canterbury four years after the meeting at Whitby. The task before him was that of organization, an activity wherein Theodore displayed remarkable ability. Under his guidance the tribal bishoprics were remodeled into the diocesan structure familiar today. The individualistic Celtic monasticism gave place to a stability and common life in the religious houses similar to that of the Benedictine ideal. The deepest marks of Theodore's work, however, were in two other fields.

Much concerned with the proper education and training of the clergy, he sought to establish among the Anglo-Saxons what today is called "native leadership." Theodore's success in this aim may be judged by the fact that he himself is the last foreign archbishop in Saxon England. All twenty-four occupants of Augustine's Chair at Canterbury between Theodore and the Norman Conquest were Saxon Churchmen.

Equally important was Theodore's establishment of the practice of regulating and invigorating the Church's life by means of regular meetings or councils of clergy and leaders. We are so accustomed to the use of conference and council as the normal means of coördinating the work of the Church that it is hard to realize how much the Church suffers without them. The synodical activity, as it is called, of the Saxon Church is a long way from the present English Convocation or American Diocesan and General Conventions, but the seeds of Anglican Church government through representative synod or council are firmly rooted in these formative years. These policies of Theodore of Tarsus, more than anything else, stamped Saxon Christianity with something of the aspect of a *national* Church.

A devotional and intellectual awakening followed on the heels of this reorganization. Owing much to earlier Celtic scholarship and spiritual ideals, the cultural life of English Christianity reached heights in the eighth century that surpassed anything known in northern Europe. These were the days when monastic and cathedral schools such as those of Theodore at Canterbury, Egbert at York, and Aldhelm at Malmesbury enjoyed their greatest fame and widest influence. The revival of learning that came to the new western empire in the reign of Charlemagne was in large part the work of Saxon scholars and teachers who, like Alcuin of York, were persuaded to bring their knowledge and influence into the Frankish Kingdom.

By far the best-known figure in the Saxon renaissance was a monk of Jarrow, the Venerable Bede. Despite the fact that he spent all his life within the confines of his own abbey or its sister-house at Wearmouth, neither the range of his learning nor the breadth of his outlook was thereby diminished. Though deeply versed in the Scriptures and the writings of all the early Christian Fathers, Bede's learning was not only what men call purely theological. He knew the works of the Latin poets and grammarians of the last days of the Roman Empire, and his own earliest writings deal with poetic principles, chronology, natural history, and science. Though his biographies of St. Cuthbert and the abbots of Jarrow would alone win him fame, his greatest work is *The Ecclesiastical History of the English People.* This is the main source of knowledge of Christianity in Celtic and Saxon England, and on its own merits is one of the world's enduring pieces of historical writing. In his time, and for centuries afterward, men will be content to have their history in the form of mere chronicle, overladen with a mass of legends and miracle stories. But Bede's alert critical faculty combined with his judgment in selecting and coördinating information to produce a work in its quality far above that of medieval historians. The Anglican tradition, with its historical sense and its emphasis on sound scholarship, owes no small debt to the venerable monk of Jarrow.

## SAXON MISSIONARY ACTIVITY

IF THE heritage of Celtic scholarship inspired to some degree the Saxon intellectual renaissance, of equal importance was the inheritance of Celtic missionary ideals. The third figure illustrative of Saxon Church life is Winfrith of Crediton, known now as St. Boniface, one of the great heroes in the missionary annals of Christianity. Born in Devonshire, then part of the kingdom of the West Saxons, and trained in the school at Exeter, Boniface turned his mind, as did so many other Anglo-Saxon missionaries, toward the heathen continental homeland whence his ancestors had come in their conquest of Roman Britain. Already another Saxon, Willibrord, patron saint of the Dutch today, was laboring to convert the Frisians of the Low Countries. To him Boniface went, early in the eighth century, for training in the missionary vocation. Thence, with the blessing and support of the pope, he moved south and east into the dark forests of heathen Germany. His missionary activity, surprisingly enough in view of his achievements, was compressed into a few years of his life on the continent. Most of the time he was employed by the papacy and the kings of the Franks, assisting in the reorganization of the Frankish Church. But however able Boniface was in forwarding the designs of the popes, his heart lay with his missions in Germany and Frisia. There he spent the final years of his ministry, meeting a martyr's death at the hands of the heathen.

For Boniface and his companions no hardship or privation was too great, no risk too costly, in the evangelization of central Germany. Pushing forward among the hostile heathen tribes, they founded little settlements that were part monasteries and centers of Christian teaching, part pioneer villages in the extension of civilization to the savage peoples of the forests. Boniface built well. His most important foundations not only endured through the years of conquest and settlement, but also exercised a decisive influence in bringing Germany into the new Christian Commonwealth of Europe.

It has sometimes been said that the test of the spiritual integrity of a church is the character of its missionary activity. There is reason to rejoice that in the unceasing efforts of the Saxons, both on the continent and later among the Danish invaders in England, there has come into our heritage this heroic reminder of the kind of missionary zeal which our Christian profession demands of us today.

### THE DANISH AND NORMAN INVASIONS

THE Church in Saxon England was not without its troubled days. Worst of all, perhaps, were those in which the whole structure of society suffered from the devastating onslaughts of the Danes. Just as the Angles and Saxons had descended upon Roman Britain, so in the ninth century the heathen Norsemen assailed the coasts of Europe as far as Sicily in the Mediterranean. England, open at all points to a maritime invader, received the full weight of Norse power. Whole towns were destroyed, churches and monasteries razed, and under the repeated blows of the Danish invaders religious and civic life alike decayed.

Yet there was a toughness in Saxon England. Men like King Alfred would not be conquered. Alfred is justly praised for a successful resistance to the Danes in which he both laid the foundations for a unified kingdom and opened the way for the assimilation of the Scandinavian settlers. To Christians, however, he is the man who did most to prevent the decay of religion and scholarship in these periods of strife, and to promote the conversion of the Danes to Christianity. Alfred's labors bore fruit fifty years later when under St. Dunstan of Glastonbury, Archbishop of Canterbury in the middle of the tenth century, learning and piety again flourished in the Saxon Church.

Saxon England disappeared in a three-cornered struggle among the Danes, the Normans, and the Saxons for mastery in the island. Final victory went to the invading forces of the aggressive Duke William of Normandy in 1066. Henceforward through the Middle Ages the kings of England will claim a domain which yokes uneasily the old Saxon kingdom with duchies and provinces across the channel in' France. For good or ill, William's victory at Hastings bound up the history of England, both political and ecclesiastical, with that of western Europe.

## CONTINENTAL INFLUENCES

INEVITABLY, the coming of the Normans produced vast changes in the social and economic structure of Saxon England as well as in the patterns of its church life. The new order in Europe after the Dark Ages was a feudal order. The new factor in the reinvigorated Church of the West was the increasingly powerful papacy, already standing on the threshold of those few centuries during which it will dominate the medieval world. To these two influences, feudal and papal, the Norman conquest opened the

English Church. The effect was virtually to revolutionize the ecclesiastical side of English life.

By the standards of his own day William I was an able Christian ruler. His keen interest in the spiritual welfare of his subjects was matched by his generosity in increasing the land holdings that made up the Church's endowments. His wise choice of bishops and abbots gave the Church of England a century of strong, devoted leadership. But naturally it was Norman and not Saxon leadership. Though his policy toward the conquered Saxons was conciliatory, William turned to men of Norman birth and training when he appointed the high officers of Church and State. Thus for three generations, until Norman and Saxon elements were fused, most of England's bishops were men whose ideas were formed by continental influences.

The first of this line was William's trusted Norman churchman, Lanfranc of Bec. Appointed Archbishop of Canterbury in 1070, he had already made his mark as educator, administrator, and theologian in Normandy. The most eminent in this succession of foreign prelates was St. Anselm, Lanfranc's successor and onetime student at Bec, a monk whose piety and learning made him one of the great saints and scholars of the early Middle Ages. These men and their colleagues devoted their energies to the task of bringing the religious life of England out of the Saxon isolation that had marked it with peculiar customs and practices, as well as with a measure of insular independence. Their success was all but complete. The national aspect of the Church in England found less and less expression as the single medieval Christian Commonwealth of Europe took shape.

Externally the old Saxon Church was rapidly altered. Everywhere the little wooden churches that predominated over stone structures disappeared in the vigorous building program of the Normans. All over the countryside new stone churches raised their massive towers, the narrow windows, thick round columns, and circular arches becoming the distinguishing marks of what is called Norman architecture today. The cathedrals and abbeys of the twelfth century still suggest as much the medieval fortress as the House of God; for the Normans they served both purposes.

The finest of the new churches were those of the monastic orders. Vast Benedictine abbeys, centers of learning, arts, and crafts as well as of devotion and worship, dominated the economic and social life of towns like Glastonbury, Evesham, Peterborough, and Bury St. Edmund's. In the remote countryside the Cistercian monasteries opened the forests and fields to farming and herding. Even today the ruins of such abbeys as Fountains and Tintern convey something of the splendor of these Cistercian foundations in the wilder regions of Yorkshire and Wales.

The twelfth century was "the century of the monks." All over Europe the monastic orders, stirred by the revival of St. Benedict's rule and ideal at Cluny, and the later influence of men like St. Bernard at Clairvaux, dominated Church and society. Monastic schools were the centers of scholarship; manors and farms of the monks led in the development of a new agricultural economy. Monastic clergy filled the highest offices of the Church; monks shared with nobles and knights the legal administration of feudal states. Time will see the decline of the monastic institution, and the decay of its ideal of sacrifice and service for the Kingdom of God. Its evangelistic spirit will pass to the preaching friars of St. Francis and St. Dominic; learning will move from monkish schools to the new universities, while lay lawyers will ultimately control the legal and political life of Europe. But this was still hidden in the unforeseen future when Lanfranc's reforms renewed the spiritual discipline and sense of vocation in the old Saxon religious houses, setting them on the path to the finest achievement of the English monastic institution in the Middle Ages.

## FEUDALISM AND THE ENGLISH CHURCH

POSSIBLY no change brings home so effectively the impact in England of the forces at work in European society as that which altered the aspect of the chief minister of the Church, the bishop. The Saxon bishop was primarily the leader among his clergy, the chief shepherd of his flock. As he traveled the roadless forests and fens of pre-conquest England, much of the apostolic character of the episcopal office must have been plain to his people. The hardship of the evangelistic mission, the demands of pastoral care, and a simplicity of life were his lot. However much in later Saxon days bishops were burdened by tasks of administration and government, the model of episcopal life and activity was still St. Cuthbert; the bishop's guide remained the ancient *Regula Pastoralis* of Pope Gregory who had sent St. Augustine to England.

But feudalism turned the bishop of Norman England into a great lord. He was the ecclesiastical superior of his clergy rather than their spiritual leader, the ruler of his flock rather than their devoted shepherd. As the Middle

Ages wore on, the bishop became a remote autocrat, absent in the service of the crown, ruling his diocese through a hierarchy of officials, his closest point of contact with both clergy and people being the fearsome one of their judge in the Church courts. Yet it is difficult to see how this unhappy element in medieval episcopacy could have been avoided.

The feudal order was based on an interlocking system of privileges and lordship, tenure of which was held by the rendering of services due from the inferior vassal to the immediate feudal overlord. From emperor down to the humblest petty squire, European society was held together by the sanctity of the oaths of loyalty that a man received from those below him, and gave in turn to those above.

The land endowments of the Church were as much a part of the system as the territories of earls and barons, a system in which there was no absolute right of private property as it is known today. Only as bishops and abbots became ecclesiastical barons, holding the Church's manors and properties subject to the rendering of homage similar to that of knights and nobles did it seem possible for the Church to maintain itself in a feudal order of society. Today this system seems to place the bishop at an immense disadvantage, mixing the things of God so inextricably with the things of Caesar that worldliness was bound to be the besetting sin of the higher clergy. Yet this was probably the only possible adjustment of the Church to the feudal system. In fact, whatever it may have done to tarnish the apostolic ideal of the episcopal office, it did meet the primary task of relating the Church to the life of the nation. We are so accustomed to think of relating the individual to the Church that we often forget that the redemptive influence of Christianity must find its way into the institutions of the social order in which man lives.

## THE MEDIEVAL CANON LAW

ANOTHER change which affected not only the bishop's office but also the very nature of the relation of Church and society, was the development of the new Canon or Church Law. The twelfth century saw the expansion of the canonical regulations governing Christian society. Side by side with the civil code of Europe and England's peculiar common law, ran the law of the Church, the development of which was examined in Chapter Two. Everywhere the canon law had won recognition by the secular authorities of the feudal states. All conceded the principle that it was within the jurisdiction of the universal Church to legislate for those areas of man's life where there was a distinctively Christian discipline to be applied. The only difficulty, and this was often a major one, was to find agreement between the civil and ecclesiastical authorities on where the powers of one ceased and the other began.

In recognition of this principle William I and Lanfranc separated the civil or royal courts from those of the Church, a distinction which had not been made clearly in Saxon England. Henceforth two systems of courts existed side by side. Royal courts administered the king's law while Church courts applied the canonical code, brought in developed form by Lanfranc from Normandy and continuously expanding in medieval England.

We are familiar today with the right of a church to

regulate its own internal life. Matters of administration, worship, the discipline of its clergy, the requirements of communicant membership—these are regarded as the proper concern of a religious body and no business of those outside its membership. But in the Middle Ages no one except the Jew and the Infidel was outside the membership of the universal Church. Canon law concerned itself not only with ecclesiastical regulations and with witchcraft and heresy, crimes of spiritual treason, but also with numerous matters that affected the daily lives of men and women. Many are those which modern society regards as the concern of the state. Matrimonial difficulties, economic regulations, probate of wills and testamentary causes, scandal, drunkenness, fornication and other moral offenses—these involved Christian discipline. Offenders and litigants were summoned to the archdeacon's court, a kind of district court, and thence if necessary to the bishop's court. Well-financed appeals might find their way before the archbishop, or even to Rome, but in ordinary cases the principals found themselves abiding by the bishop's judgment or lodged in the episcopal dungeon.

## THE CONFLICT OF CHURCH AND STATE

LITTLE imagination is required to see that these two changes—the appearance of the bishop as a feudal baron, and the recognition of a separate legal jurisdiction in the Church courts—contained the seeds of bitter conflict between Church and State. Indeed, much of medieval history is simply the story of these conflicts.

The bishop's double status of temporal baron and spiritual minister, for example, raised to vital importance the manner of his appointment. Who shall select the bishop? His superior as a temporal baron, the king? Or his superior as a spiritual officer, the pope? By whose power is he installed into possession of his diocese? Kings and overlords could scarcely relinquish their claims to fill vacant sees. Often the manors and properties of the bishopric constituted a feudal barony larger and richer than that of the neighboring knights and earls. The very integrity of the feudal state thus depended upon the return of the same loyalty and services to the crown by the ecclesiastical baron as by the lay nobleman. Yet on the other hand, it was essential to the freedom of the Church that its endowments be protected against confiscation and its bishops be men faithful to their spiritual obligations.

Here was an impasse that only compromise could resolve. In the conflict between king and pope the ancient rights of the people to choose their chief shepherd vanished. Cathedral chapters elected the royal nominee or the papal candidate, in accordance with an arrangement between king and pope in which the conflicts inherent in the situation were normally avoided. St. Anselm, Lanfranc's successor, after a violent quarrel with William II, devised an arrangement with Henry I whereby king and pope divided between them the symbolic actions by which a bishop was installed in his see. The crown would receive the bishop's homage, investing him in return with the temporal possessions of the diocese; the Church would place the pastoral staff in his hands, sign of his spiritual power and authority. Thus England anticipated the same compromise which concluded the long investiture struggle already witnessed between the Emperor Henry IV and

Pope Gregory VII. The bishop was the king's man in respect to the temporal powers and properties of the see; he was the pope's man in respect to his ecclesiastical loyalty. The only question that remained and, of course, the ultimate one, was which power was superior to the other and held directly of God, the temporal *regnum* of the king or the spiritual *sacerdotium* of the pope?

As noted in the previous chapter, Europe received its answer to that question in the theories developed by the champions of papal supremacy on the continent. This answer was unmistakably communicated to the English by Thomas Becket, Archbishop of Canterbury, whose murder ended one of the bitterest conflicts of Church and State in medieval England.

## THOMAS BECKET AND HENRY II

THE struggle between Becket and Henry II was over the canon law. Where did the power of the Church court end and that of the royal court begin? Each had well-recognized spheres, but between the two was a kind of legal no-man's land where both made claims. In the days of a strong monarch, such as William the Conqueror, the king's law was unchallenged. But in times of political chaos the Church managed to extend her jurisdiction at the expense of the royal prerogative.

In 1154, after a period of eighteen years of civil strife, Henry II came to the throne with a resolute determination to restore the royal authority to the point to which it had been raised by his forefathers. The independence of the feudal barons could be curbed with relative ease, but when he attacked the power of the Church, even under the plea of returning to the ancient customs in England, Henry found an antagonist he could not defeat.

The immediate battleground of the king and archbishop was the claim of the Church to deal with criminals among the clergy without interference from the secular authorities, a canonical privilege known as *benefit of clergy*. The king did not challenge the right of the Church to try a cleric accused of crime, but he insisted that those found guilty should be turned over to his courts for punishment under the king's law. To Henry, expending all his energies in rebuilding the legal and judicial system of England, it seemed a monstrous injustice that the crimes of murder, rape, and robbery carried death or fearful multilation to the ordinary man, while the cleric who committeed these offences might receive a flogging or be thrown into an episcopal prison whence escape was all too easy. The king insisted that the supreme penalty of the Church courts, degradation from holy orders, should be inflicted on guilty clerics, after which the secular courts would mete out to them the same punishment received by laymen.

To Becket, this was to punish a man twice for the same crime. Degradation might seem a light sentence to us, but in the twelfth century men were far more conscious than we of the eternal punishment the unrepentant sinner would meet in the next world. The archbishop's strenuous and stubborn opposition to the king's legal reforms was aroused at bottom by the threat they contained to the independent power of an international Church.

Beyond the matter of the courts, Henry's codification of the ancient customs touched other sore points. He proposed, for example, that no appeals should be made to Rome without his consent, a demand that would virtually allow the crown to determine just how much effective power the pope could exert in the English Church. He would further define the control of the king over appointments to bishoprics as well as over the temporalities of those sees. Becket saw clearly that these and other claims of Henry would place the king "in the Pope's stead" in England, enslaving the Church, as he thought, to the State. He answered the ultimate question involved in these conflicts in plain language.

"The Church of Christ," he wrote, while in temporary exile, "is constituted of two orders: the Clergy and the People, the one having the care of the Church that all may be ruled for the salvation of souls; the other consisting of kings, princes, and nobles who carry on the secular government that all things may lead to the peace and unity of the Church. It is certain that kings receive their power from the Church, and the Church not from them but from Christ. . . ."

There could be no reconciliation between Henry II and Thomas Becket. One must give way. Twice in English history the clash of these conflicting principles came to the breaking-point. In this, the first instance, the king was defeated. Becket, murdered in Canterbury Cathedral in 1170 by a band of knights who thought they did their king a service, accomplished in martyrdom what he could not do in life. The wave of horror which swept over Christendom after the bloody deed carried the canon law to final victory in England, and St. Thomas of Canterbury to the position of the most popular saint of the Middle Ages.

Four hundred years later the clash will come again under Henry VIII, strangely like his ancestor Henry II. Victory will go then to the crown. But four centuries will see all the circumstances changed: king, clergy, and people alike will unite in repudiating the claims of an alien papal authority over their national Church. If the plundering and destruction of the great shrine of St. Thomas Becket at Canterbury was one of the least admirable acts of Henry VIII, at least it indicated that monarch had some historical knowledge. No one could have devised a more striking symbol of the rejection of the papal canon law.

Right or wrong, Becket was one of the great medieval figures of the English Church. His single-minded, unswerving devotion to duty, and his courage unto death earned him the acclaim and veneration of the common people as the champion of the supremacy of the things of God over those of Caesar. As long as the English language endures, his finest memorial will be the stream of pilgrims, wending their reminiscent way to his shrine in Chaucer's *Canterbury Tales.*

## ENGLAND AND THE PAPACY

PAPAL power in England reached its height in the century that followed the martyrdom of Thomas Becket. Innocent III, enjoying the full papal power described in an earlier chapter,[2] not only forced King John to halt his interference with the affairs and property of the Church, but also received from that unhappy monarch the acknowledgment that he held even his crown at the pleasure of the

[2] See pages 76-77.

papacy. Though the feudal tribute that symbolized this papal overlordship rankled in the minds of Englishmen for several generations, Innocent's successors at Rome were not slow to take advantage of the power bequeathed to them. Papal taxation of the wealth of the English Church increased enormously in the thirteenth and fourteenth centuries, while the claim of the popes to appoint their nominees to ecclesiastical positions in England was realized again and again.

It is difficult to know which of these practices aroused the anger of Englishmen more. The army of papal collectors was detested everywhere. While the vast sums that poured out of England into the papal coffers were drawn from the incomes of the Church, yet it was part of the national wealth, and its expenditure in the political designs of popes was often hostile to English interests on the continent. Similarly, while men opposed the pope's extension of his power to fill vacancies in the English Church by appealing to local rights of appointment that had come down from Saxon days, they did so the more bitterly because many of the bishoprics and important benefices were bestowed upon foreigners who enjoyed the incomes without ever setting foot in England.

The same forces that aroused men against the papacy on the continent were at work in late medieval England. The difference was that in the island kingdom they found speedier expression. England had never moved easily in the continental imperial system, and a coherent national self-consciousness was bred by her isolation. Long before the forces of nationalism split the Medieval Commonwealth of Europe into sovereign states, England had become a nation. Thus her growing resentment of the papacy was not an objection to the spiritual authority of Rome in the Catholic Church, but to an alien interference with English rights and customs, English property and interests.

Here, at least, is part of the reason why, when the Reformation came, the repudiation of a foreign papal authority was an act with which virtually the whole nation identified itself. Henry VIII began where Henry II stood, but in the centuries between the Normans and the Tudors England had developed an intensely self-conscious national life. Thus at the outset the quarrel between Henry VIII and the pope was primarily political rather than religious, and precisely that foreshadowed in medieval England. It was a quarrel with an alien power whose claims and whose law ran counter to the interests of the English nation.

## ANTIPAPAL LEGISLATION

RESENTMENT of the papacy in the fourteenth century found expression in a series of parliamentary statutes, passed in an attempt to curb the unlimited use of the pope's power in matters not purely religious. It is noteworthy that the first of these ordinances was passed in the reign of Edward I, exactly at the time when the humiliation of Pope Boniface VIII by the King of France gave warning that the new nations of Europe had little respect for papal pretensions to universal temporal sovereignty. Equally significant is the date of the most stringent of these limitations on Rome's claims. They coincide with the residence of the popes in Avignon, where the financial and moral corruption of the papal court, as well as its subservience to the French king, dealt the prestige of the popes a severe blow.

The precise content of these statutes is not of great importance to us. They were never strictly enforced. Parliamentary ordinances in fourteenth-century England did not have the legislative force they later acquired, being rather more like resolutions than laws, registrations of protest that might serve as useful weapons for the royal policy at the moment. What is important is the very fact of their passage and the use made of them in Reformation England. The men of Tudor England will look back to this medieval legislation and find their justification for their assertion of the ancient independence of England in matters of Church and State alike.

## THE CHANGING SCENE

THE rise of nationalism was the chief change in the European political scene in the two centuries before the Reformation. But in addition, the fourteenth and fifteenth centuries witnessed economic and social changes quite as revolutionary as those in English political life. Feudalism died out, its political significance gone when a strong, centralized monarchy stripped the barons of their independence; its economic system no longer workable when the new merchant classes dominated the towns and trades, while the new free yeoman-farmer took the place of the old serf on the feudal manor. The rise of the middle classes, destined to become the backbone of English society, was perhaps the most important social change in pre-Reformation England. To these classes the ecclesiastical institution often seemed to prevent progress in the new capitalist economy. The man of the Renaissance sought emancipation from the old restrictions in the world of trade and commerce quite as much as in the world of art and learning. Before him the Church stood entrenched, enormously wealthy, controlling vast acres of the richest manors and farms in England, and blocking the expansion of the new economy.

Important as are these political and economic changes in understanding the causes of the Reformation, there remains the religious factor, that is, the discontent within the life of the Church itself. In the complexity of medieval society it is difficult to disentangle these factors from each other, except for convenience of discussion. Religion on the eve of the Reformation is still inseparable from politics and prices.

The clamor for reform in the Church reached its height in the great Church councils of the early fifteenth century. There "Reform in head and members!" was the cry. Seeking some principle of unity which would hold the Christian West together in the face of the new separate national allegiances, men proposed to reform the constitution of the Church. In place of the autocratic papacy, supreme authority would be vested in the General Council of which the pope would become the chief administrative servant. But the nationalism that was strong enough to defy the ancient prestige and power of a monarchical papacy could scarcely be expected to give way before the cumbersome machinery of a council. The Conciliar Movement failed of nearly all its aims, but the discontent with the Church and the zeal of reformers was not abated.

## ECCLESIASTICAL EVILS AND ABUSES

MANY of the abuses against which this cry for reform was raised are better described as ecclesiastical than religious. The exorbitant financial exactions of the papacy, the continued interference of Rome in matters that were increasingly regarded as the domestic concerns of the national Church, and the impossibility of securing speedy and fair decisions in the ecclesiastical courts inflamed all Europe. However loyal to the Church, men felt at every turn the friction between the old canon law and the new claims of the developing modern state. The anti-clericalism, widespread in the century before the Reformation, was in part the natural reaction of new groups in society, struggling for self-realization, and bidding for power and influence against the vast array of benefits and immunities enjoyed by the privileged clerical class.

There is no question that abuses were real, and in many cases unendurable. The Renaissance papacy had lost all semblance of moral and spiritual integrity. Popes were frankly secular princes, using the resources entrusted to them for the welfare of Christendom to further their political and personal ambitions in Italy. Under men like Alexander VI, father of the notorious Lucrezia Borgia, who was made pope in the year Columbus discovered America, the iniquity and immorality of Rome became a by-word in northern Europe.

It is not surprising that corruption at the center of the Church's life was reflected in all its branches. The monastic orders had long since declined from their original ideal. Bishops, more often than not employed in the government service of monarchs, ruled their dioceses from a distance, assisted by a vast army of rapacious officials. Among the lower clergy, Church offices and preferments were openly sought and bought. It was not uncommon for a man to be rector of several parishes and ministering in none of them. Instead, he lived on their revenues at court or in some other post, while a priest hired by him at starvation wages provided the minimum of pastoral care for the neglected parishioners. Often parishes were handed over to bankrupt monasteries that the monks might recoup their finances out of the tithes, with little thought for the spiritual needs of the people. While the occasional conscientious bishop might do something to reform the scandals of ignorance and immorality that were common among his clergy, he was powerless to attack these other abuses. Men flaunted his authority with a papal dispensation which allowed their evil practices and placed them beyond episcopal control.

## RELIGION IN PRE-REFORMATION ENGLAND

No CRY of the reformers was more insistent than their condemnation of the superstitious practices that the Church suffered to exist as the religion of the ordinary man. By and large, despite exaggerations, the charges of the reformers were well-founded. Pious observances and customs, once the inspiration to deeper devotion, had become changed out of all recognition. Pardons and indulgences remitting the punishments of purgatory were commonly sold, along with the miraculous charms, bones, and trinkets that passed as relics of the saints. Veneration of such relics reached the pitch of absurdity when men looked with awe upon the ashes of Moses' burning bush, or goggled before a handful of the very earth out of which Adam was created! Pilgrimages to the popular shrines of Thomas Becket at Canterbury, Our Lady of Walsingham, or St. David of Wales, if less frequent than in earlier years, were also less pious. At best an innocent holiday junket in the name of religion, the pilgrimage was a painless way of sharing in the treasury of merit.

Much of the superstition of medieval folk was due to their ignorance. More than a little of their pagan heritage was still with them. Their world was peopled with witches and sorcerers; devils lurked in the forests and rode on the storms; the "Little People" of the earth were their mischievous enemies. It is no wonder that the old woman in the village stole the consecrated host from the altar to scatter over her garden as a charm against worms, or that others relied upon the potent protection of holy water.

It is often said that few of these superstitions were actually evil, and the greater number quite innocent. One might speak with equal truth concerning the religious practices of heathen tribes in Africa. The majority of these superstitions were quite irrelevant to Christianity. The real point is not how harmful they were in themselves, but the place they occupied in the religion of the ordinary man. The harm they did was to provide him with a set of semi-pagan, superstitious external practices in the place of the means to a constant self-offering in the companionship of Christ which is the heart of the Gospel. Any substitute for that, whether the foolish fancies of the medieval man or the more reprehensible follies of the modern materialist, is a form of idolatry. No one will maintain that the Reformation succeeded in destroying men's idols entirely, but the reformers were at least right in holding the Church accountable.

The Church may not have been responsible for the semi-pagan climate which surrounded medieval life, but there is a wide difference between endeavoring to eradicate that climate and adjusting Christianity to it. Yet medieval man still moved in a world of superstition inside his Church as well as outside. He viewed the mystery performed by the priest at the altar as a kind of supreme magical rite. Here was the magic of God, confounding the powers of evil that sought to wrest his soul to damnation. The folk of the Middle Ages lived close to the horizon between this world and the next, so close that the next world often had more reality than this one. As they stood in the parish church the lurid paintings on the walls reminded them of the eternal future. There in crude detail were depicted the bliss of the saved in Paradise and the agonized torments of the damned in Hell. But over all hung the rood, the crucifix of Christ's passion, the one thing that made the difference in men's destiny. The power of that saving act of Christ on the cross was brought down to the altar as the priest celebrated the mysterious act of the Mass.

The difficulty was perhaps less with the theology than with that point where the Christian faith had its impact in the mind and heart of the believer. If he were obedient to the laws and precepts of the Church, the victory won by Christ on the cross was extended to him through the sacraments, but the transaction was a mechanical one. It made few demands for a faith that was the response of the whole man in trust and love and self-dedication to his Divine Companion.

For the religious ignorance of men the Church was directly responsible. Nothing brings home so sharply the contrasts in medieval life as the wide gap between the learning of the educated few and the ignorance of the illiterate masses. However well the university scholar or the higher cleric knew his Bible, among most of the inferior clergy and their village parishioners knowledge of the Scriptures was rare. Even possession of parts of the Bible in the vulgar tongue was sternly condemned by the ecclesiastical authorities, lest the simple fall into heresy through misinterpretation of the Word of God.

The stories told in church paintings or stained glass, together with the scenes enacted in the popular miracle plays, have sometimes been called "the Bible of the poor." But even these were so overladen with legend that they would scarcely be recognized as biblical today. Despite repeated injunctions by his superiors, the parish priest in rural England gave little formal religious instruction. The occasional visit of a wandering friar was almost certain to bring an arresting sermon, larded with racy anecdotes and pointed up with a simple moral, but the vicar's usual homily was more likely to be concerned with the payment of tithe than with the knowledge of God.

The most serious spiritual impoverishment of medieval religious life was the inability of the ordinary man to participate in the chief service of his Church, the Holy Communion or Mass. Not only was the Latin language an effective barrier between him and the meaning of the sacrament, but the popular notion that the Mass was an act performed by the priest on behalf of the people restricted him to the murmuring of an *Ave Maria* or *Pater Noster* while the supreme corporate act of Christian worship was reduced to recitation by one man. The outreaching and evangelizing power of the liturgy was thus denied the majority of medieval folk. Lacking the highest means of that self-offering of the whole man to God which is the essence of all true worship, it is not surprising that he sought release in a multitude of superstitious beliefs and practices.

ATTEMPTS AT REFORM

THE last decades of the fifteenth and the opening years of the sixteenth centuries witnessed determined attempts to end the worst of the ecclesiastical and religious abuses. Cardinal Ximenes laid a very heavy hand upon the corruption and decay in the Spanish Church; Nicholas of Cusa strove to reform the monasteries in Germany and Austria. Savonarola thundered his denunciations of the Renaissance papacy from his pulpit in Florence; Erasmus divided his time between a satirical exposure of the follies and evils in the Church's life and a valiant effort to bring men back to the New Testament and the theology of the Fathers of the Early Church.

In England the line of *Catholic Reformers,* as they are called by historians, was a distinguished one: Cardinal Morton with his monastic reforms; Archbishop Warham, Thomas More, Bishop Fisher of Rochester, patrons of the Christian New Learning; Erasmus, gentlest of the satirists and greatest of the scholars; and John Colet, Dean of St. Paul's, whose lectures on St. Paul at Oxford did much to revolutionize the study of the New Testament and free it from the fixed and artificial methods of scriptural interpretation common in the late Middle Ages. But these men were too late and too few to stem the drift toward violent change.

A final aspect of Christianity in pre-Reformation England remains to be noted. One of the imperishable strains of Christian religious experience has been the repeated yearning of men for a simple evangelical fellowship in which life is guided by the Gospel precepts, and each man finds a discipleship like that of the little company that walked the Galilean roads with the Master. Over and over again in Christian history this strain has broken out, challenging the worldliness of the institutional Church, witnessing against compromise with the encroachments of secularism. It appeared in the earliest days when Montanus and his followers found the institutional channels of the Church too narrow for their enthusiasm. More than a little of this deep yearning formed the spiritual drive in the origin of Christian monasticism. The monks of St. Basil in the East and St. Benedict in the West, the Celtic wanderers, the bands of Saxon missionaries were all moved by it.

Even in the high Middle Ages this strain of Christian experience struggled for expression. The evangelical Waldensians, the simple companies of The Poor Men of Lyons, the first friars of St. Francis himself alike challenged the Church of Innocent III with the reminder that Gospel discipleship was that to which all things must point.

This aspect of Christian experience has had its intolerant, puritanical side. Often, and especially under persecution, it has developed peculiar aberrations, withdrawing itself from the very world where the Christian religion must live and exert its redemptive power. Often, too, what begins in this simple witness of discipleship has ended in such a distortion of faith and practice as to remove itself completely from the main stream of Christianity. The evidence of Church history seems to indicate that this perversion of what is originally a spirit very close to that of the New Testament, comes about when the Church of the moment is unable to give place and expression to the evangelical vocation; in short, when the Church is something less than fully Catholic. Such clearly was the situation in the century before the Reformation.

## JOHN WYCLIFFE

JOHN WYCLIFFE, scholar and priest, nationalist and patriot, was in many ways England's most important figure in this evangelical stream in the fourteenth century. His bitter denunciations of the Church's misuse of its wealth and power, his attack upon the sacramental system and his defiant translation of the Latin Vulgate Bible into English, caused a later generation to hail him as "The Morning Star of the Reformation." Wycliffe died in 1384, quietly in his rectory at Lutterworth, his protection from the long arm of the papacy eloquent testimony to the willingness of Englishmen to control their domestic spiritual concerns. For twenty years his zealous preachers, carrying their Scriptures to the people, denounced the evils and corruptions of the ecclesiastical institution. Only the most severe measures of the Church's repressive machinery finally drove them from the scene.

There is, however, one thing to remember about this medieval evangelicalism. Wycliffe had only a distant kinship with Reformation Protestantism. In fact, it is more by poetic license than historical accuracy that he can be called a harbinger of the Reformation. His denunciations of the corruptions of the papacy, the concern of the Church with matters temporal to the neglect of those spiritual, and the luxury and decadence of the monasteries, were all echoed by the best of orthodox medieval Churchmen. His attack upon the sacramental system was not so much a theological assault on medieval doctrine as it was a means of breaking the spiritual tyranny exercised by the ecclesiastical hierarchy over the lives of the folk. The power of the priest rested upon the fact that he alone could perform the miracle of Christ's Presence in the Sacrament of the Altar; he alone could grant or withhold the absolution that restored the sinner in the Sacrament of Penance. It was the power of the hierarchy that Wycliffe saw as a barrier to the free course of the Gospel. Even his battle for the Bible was directed by other motives than those which moved the men of the Protestant Reformation. To his followers the Gospel was a plain rule of faith and life, the simple ethical injunctions of which should be graven on the hearts of all men.

"I would have the weakest woman read the Gospels and the Epistles . . . I would have those works translated into all languages . . . I long for the man in the fields to sing them to himself as he follows the plough, the weaver to hum them to the tune of his shuttle . . ." The words are those of a Catholic reformer, Erasmus, a century and a quarter later; the spirit is that of John Wycliffe. Luther and the Protestant reformers fought their way in deep spiritual agony through the meaning of St. Paul's cry "The just shall live by faith!"—fought their way to a passionate conviction in which they overthrew the Medieval Church. But in years before the Reformation, here and there in the humble cottages or merchant's house where the influence of Wycliffe lingered, it was not the spiritual wrestlings of *The Epistle to the Romans* which touched the minds of Englishmen. They turned their treasured and well-thumbed fragments of the New Testament to *The Epistle of St. James*. The simple and practical injunctions spoke to their hearts: "Pure religion and undefiled before God and the Father is this, to visit the fatherless and widows in their affliction, and to keep himself unspotted from the world."

HERE, then, in the changing scene of the fourteenth and fifteenth centuries lie the roots of the Reformation. In different areas of Europe the forces are at work in different combinations and with varying degrees of importance. The political ones loom largest in the England of 1500. Henry VIII had no religious quarrel with a pope who had made him "Defender of the Faith," but Tudor England in its national self-consciousness had a quarrel with the interference of an alien papacy. Yet before the Reformation in England has run its course each factor in turn —political conflict, social and economic change, ecclesiastical reform, and the resurgence of the evangelical witness —has decisively affected the Anglicanism that is our heritage.

# CHAPTER FOUR

# The Crisis of the Reformation

IN THE early years of the sixteenth century the forces of change that were at work in the preceding two hundred years were at last loosed in religious revolution. So completely was the medieval papacy identified with the old order that inevitably the Reformation involved rebellion against the papal principle and all the institutions that embodied it. However much the reformers differed from each other in their attempts to restore to the Church the faith and practice of its primitive days, on one thing they were agreed: the papacy had no warrant either in Scripture or in the history of early Christianity.

Once allegiance to the papacy had been repudiated, the Reformation followed its different paths in Germany, Switzerland, England, and other areas of Europe. Social, economic, and political movements exercised their influence upon the course of religious reform, and were of no small importance in shaping the separate Churches that emerged from the century or more of crisis.

When the storm had passed, Lutheran Protestantism differed from Calvinism. The radical sects differed still more from both. There was little left in many parts of the continent of Europe that bore much outward semblance to western Catholicism on the eve of the Reformation. Even the Church of Rome, markedly altered by a Catholic Revival that was partly stimulated by the Protestant Reformation, presented a different face to the world. The dogmatic rigidity and narrowness of temper that characterized Romanism after the Council of Trent seemed to have little in common with the old Renaissance Catholicism.

Among them all the character of the Church of England after the Reformation was unique. Anglicanism, properly speaking, is a product of the experience of the English Church in this crisis, but it is quite unintelligible if it is isolated from the earlier history of Christianity in England. There was an essential continuity in the life of the Church of England before and after the Reformation. In that lies much of the unique character of the modern English Church. Anglicanism preserved its Catholic heritage even as it rediscovered the evangelical witness of the Gospel.

### THE REVOLT IN GERMANY

IT WAS not mere accident that the flame of the Reformation was ignited first in Germany. There all the vast changes of the Renaissance had received less opportunity for expression than elsewhere in northern Europe. The new national self-consciousness which stirred the Germans as well as other European peoples had little chance of realization as long as the Germanic states were linked with half of Europe in the uneasy yoke of the Hapsburg Empire. The grievances of the new middle classes were bitter. In no other area of Europe had trade and commerce, craftsmanship and merchandising, made so many advances, and yet the stubborn hold of the old feudal structure of society gave little recognition to these folk who were destined to be the builders of the modern world.

The lot of the peasant-serf was worse. England already had seen the gradual social changes that turned the feudal serf into the independent yeoman-farmer over a hundred years before. France, in the grip of a strong central monarchy, managed to postpone that upheaval until the change was telescoped into the brief, bloody days of the French Revolution. But in Germany this social unrest coincided with the Reformation. The radical sects of the religious revolution found thousands of eager adherents among the poor and the peasant of the depressed classes.

Throughout the Germanic states the Church was identified with the forces of reaction. On nearly every front the ecclesiastical authorities opposed the influences of the Renaissance. As a result, earnest Catholic reformers could accomplish little or nothing. The new Christian biblical and historical scholarship was vehemently condemned. Religious abuses and corruption in Church life were widespread. Many of the extensive bishoprics of Germany, for example, were virtually independent states, their prelates ruling as secular princes with little concern for the spiritual welfare of the flock of Christ.

IN THIS situation there was needed only an occasion that would uncover the explosive material and a leader who would ignite the spark of protest. Both appeared in 1517. The occasion was the sale of an indulgence issued by Pope Leo X. The leader was an Augustinian monk and scholar named Martin Luther. On October 31 of that year, Luther, aroused in passionate protest against the superstitious practices associated with the system of indulgences, nailed to the door of the Wittenberg Church his open challenge to these abuses of the Christian doctrine of forgiveness.

The indulgence had long been an accepted part of the Church's penitential system. The contrite sinner was assigned in the confessional some act of reparation or penance to perform. He did it both as a sign of his sincere repentance and a symbol of the earthly or temporal punishment sin deserves. This act of discipline could in no way affect the sinner's guilt before God. Only true contrition could bring the divine forgiveness that saved the sinner from eternal punishment. But earthly consequences must be borne even by the forgiven, and the Church on earth claimed the power to regulate these temporal penances. In return, therefore, for some act of piety or charity, the Church might cancel the penance laid upon the sinner in this life or yet to be fulfilled in purgatory. Such an indulgence was issued to those who performed a specified act of devotion or charity. In theory, the indulgence could apply only to the contrite and absolved sinner. In practice, it had come to be thought of as an easier way to forgiveness than the hard road of true repentance.

Leo X issued his indulgences to all who would contribute to the papal building program at Rome. Luther saw his people flocking to buy the indulgence certificates with the notion that they would thereby escape the consequences of wrong-doing. In the popular mind this transaction freed a man from the consequences of sin both in this life and in the hereafter, and true repentance fell into the background as men and women relied upon the merits of the indulgence. Moreover, the indulgence-preachers did little to combat the widespread idea that "as soon as money in the coffer rings, the soul from purgatory's fire springs!"

Thanks to the new printing press, Luther's challenge was speedily debated everywhere in western Europe. In the midst of the clamor that arose Luther perceived with remarkable clarity that the indulgence dispute was quite insignificant. The corruptions of the medieval system stood together as a whole. They rested upon a single foundation: the papal institution. Emerging from his biblical and historical studies with the zeal of a prophet, Luther made his sweeping appeal from the authority of the pope to the authority of Holy Scripture. Against the whole mechanical scheme of salvation by outward, formal obedience to the Church's precepts, Luther asserted the sole supremacy of the response of faith in the heart of the believer.

*Salvation came by faith alone.* Nothing could shake Luther from this burning conviction. Disputations, threats, and dangers left him unmoved. Protected by powerful friends among the petty German princes, he defied the pope and the Catholic emperor. Overnight Luther became the hero of his nation, and to thousands of German people the incorruptible man of God. Amid the cheers of the Wittenberg students, he burned the papal bull which condemned him, casting into the same fire the code of canon law upon which the claims of papal power rested. The structure of the Medieval Church in Luther's Germany was rapidly being swept away.

## LUTHERAN DOCTRINE

MARTIN LUTHER's three most influential books came from his pen in 1520. A brief consideration of them will indicate many of the distinctive lines followed by Protestantism in the years of the Reformation.

*On the Babylonish Captivity of the Church* contained Luther's attack upon the sacramental system of the Medieval Church. According to Luther, the true sacraments are those actions which are charged with the biblical promise of divine grace. Only to such promises of God can man respond in faith. Baptism, Penance, and the Lord's Supper are the real sacraments in the body of Christ's faithful. Each must be rescued from the "captivity" in which the corruptions of the papal Church held it.

Formalism, for example, has obscured the tremendous significance of the new birth into faith that Baptism signifies. Penance must again recover its primary emphasis upon true repentance in the heart of the sinner who can plead only the grace and faith that brings him humbly to seek forgiveness. The Lord's Supper must be freed from the evil doctrine of transubstantiation, and from the view that the Mass itself is a good work in performing which man can earn merit in the eyes of God. The holy communion with God whereby the faithful man receives the strengthening Body and Blood of his Divine Companion must again be recognized as the central meaning of the Mass.

Once attacked, the sacramental system was subjected to an increasing variety of interpretation. Luther and his conservative followers maintained a very real hold upon the activity of God in and through the sacraments. The radical groups, however, that mushroomed up around the fringes of the Protestant revolt regarded the sacraments as formal pledges of God's favor or ceremonies of human inspiration. Luther saw no objection to retaining much that was valuable in the old forms of devotion and worship, though undoubtedly he shifted their emphasis, and in some cases, their meaning. All that was not specifically forbidden in Holy Scripture might lawfully be retained. Such was his general principle. For this reason the Lutheran reformed Mass, now a communion service in the German vernacular, remained surrounded by much of the ancient beauty and traditional ceremonies of medieval worship.

Among the more radical sects the break with the past was complete. Infrequently celebrated, the Lord's Supper became a memorial service of solemn remembrance of Jesus' last meal with His disciples. Churches were stripped of their traditional ornaments. Organs, statues, vestments, altars, stained glass, and sacred vessels were destroyed. All that was not specifically enjoined in Holy Scripture was unlawful for a true Christian. Thus men were launched into the central problem of authority that tortured the reformers for a century and more. To set up Scripture as the sole authority is to separate the Bible from the life of the Church. Who then is to interpret the Scripture aright?

Luther's tract *Concerning Christian Liberty* contains his central doctrine of justification by faith. Salvation rests upon man's faith alone. In understanding Luther, it must be remembered that his conception of faith was far richer than that achieved by most of his followers. Faith, according to Luther, is the mighty operation of God's spirit in man's heart, arousing in him an unwavering trust in God's love for him. In this trust man commits himself wholly to God, relying upon no merit of his own, but only upon the redemption Christ has wrought for us in God's love.

On such faith rests man's spiritual liberty. United with Christ in this self-commitment of faith, the Christian shares in the kingship and priesthood of Jesus. The believer is "lord of all," as Luther put it. Yet at the same time he is "servant of all" because he shares the Master's vocation of service as he shares His kingship. Indeed, the kingship is one of brotherly love and service to man.

### THE CHARACTER OF LUTHERANISM

IT WAS this assertion of the essential priesthood of all believers that swept the historic Catholic conception of the Church's ministry out of Lutheranism. Apostolic succession and the hierarchy of ministers became meaningless. Spiritual powers were not indelibly conferred upon men at ordination. Lutheran pastors were representatives of the people, called and commissioned to be Ministers of the Word and Sacraments on behalf of them all. They exercised a ministerial function which, though endowed with spiritual power, was at bottom common to all faithful believers.

The form of the ministry was, therefore, of secondary interest in Lutheran Protestantism. It varied from place to place. In some areas of Germany and in Denmark, for example, the old title of bishop was retained to describe the new administrative superintendents of the Lutheran congregations. The temporal powers of the Catholic bishops passed readily into the hands of the Lutheran princes. The former episcopal sacramental functions ceased to have any place in church life.

In Sweden alone among the Lutheran State Churches the historic episcopal succession was preserved, largely through the conversion of the Bishop of Westeras to the reformed religion. To this day the Church of Sweden possesses an episcopate in unbroken continuity with its bishops of the Middle Ages. The fact that this is of purely secondary interest in Lutheranism is clearly shown by the full communion which the Swedish Church enjoys with other non-episcopal Lutheran bodies. The essential bond of unity is not the historic episcopate, but the distinctive Lutheran doctrines.

The third of Luther's important writings was his *Address to the Christian Nobility* in which he summons the Christian princes of Germany to undertake the reform so urgently needed in Christendom.

Luther's appeal to the State has often been misunderstood. While it resulted in the establishment of Lutheran State Churches in those areas of Germany and Scandinavia where Protestantism triumphed, Martin Luther was far from intending to reduce the Church to control by the secular authorities or make it the creature of the State. He was concerned with restoring to Christian princes their religious functions. To him the civil power was not *secular;* that is, having no relation to God's governance of His created world of men. It was *sacred;* that is, in some sense God-given and divinely ordained. Here Luther stood squarely in a tradition that sprang from the Bible and was commonly accepted in the centuries before the papacy had claimed all power for itself. In that tradition temporal authority was as much of a sacred trust as any spiritual power.

The petty princes of Germany were not interested in the origins and obligations of the spiritual functions that Luther ascribed to them. But they were attracted by the new political power which Lutheranism brought them. They grasped eagerly at the opportunity to free themselves from both the papacy and the Catholic emperor.

Luther had no notion that one day his affirmation of the sacredness of civil power would enslave the German Church to the dictates of a purely secular or even anti-Christian state. While the beginnings of the modern totalitarian state may be found in the sixteenth century or even before, it is well to remember that the reformers could not imagine a society not undergirded by Christian principles.

### LUTHERANISM RECOGNIZED

By 1530 Lutheranism was strong enough in many of the German States to challenge the Catholic empire itself. In that year the *Confession of Augsburg,* in which the Lutheran doctrines were enshrined, was presented to the imperial assembly. The Catholic princes secured its condemnation, but Lutheran strength was too stubbornly intrenched to accept the verdict. Consequently, the years that followed were ones of bitter civil war between Catholic and Protestant States. It was a conflict in which rebellion, intrigue, and the ambitions of the various rulers played as large a part as the issue of religious division.

Peace was temporarily found in 1555. Exhausted by the struggle, the princes engineered a settlement in which the recognition of Lutheranism was won from the Catholics. The German principalities that adhered to the *Confession of Augsburg* were allowed liberty in respect to their beliefs and practices. But no one could yet conceive toleration on other than a territorial scale. It was quite unthinkable that within a given state there should be differences in religion. The basis of this precarious settlement, therefore, was the famous principle that in each tiny principality the religion of the prince was to be the religion of his people. Those who differed from their rulers were forced either to conform or to emigrate to the nearest territory of their religious allegiance.

Neither the principle of freedom of conscience nor any mature concept of religious toleration was embodied in this uneasy truce. Though Lutheranism and Catholicism enjoyed territorial recognition, no other religious body could be tolerated. Moreover, the struggle of the princes to emancipate themselves from the imperial interference would still go on. The new commercial and middle classes would continue to strive for their share of power in the new order. The religious conflict was made to serve the interests and ambitions of both.

As Germany drifted toward a new and more intense outbreak of the wars of religion, it became evident that Lutheranism, confined to the German and Scandinavian states, lacked the dynamic to play the major role in the new Protestantism. The forces of international Protestantism centered in the Calvinism of the Swiss Reformation.

## THE REFORMATION IN SWITZERLAND

ALMOST simultaneously with the Lutheran revolt, the clamor for reform was heard in Switzerland. Huldreich Zwingli, the people's priest at the Great Minster in Zurich, led the rebellion against the authority of the Bishop of Constance in whose diocese Zurich was located.

By 1525 Zwingli's evangelical principles had captured the whole Swiss canton. Church properties were confiscated, much of the money being devoted to the foundation of schools. Convents and monastic houses were dissolved, churches stripped of all the externals of Catholic worship, and every shred of the old ecclesiastical authority was destroyed. The local government in the little Swiss city-state directed and controlled the reform program. The city councillors of Zurich, under the influence of Zwingli and his ministers, solemnly declared Holy Scripture to be the sole source of Christian doctrine as well as the only guide to church discipline and practice. Bible lectures and evangelical services in the vernacular replaced the old forms of worship. The new *Order of the Communion* prescribed a memorial service of utmost simplicity.

Spreading rapidly to other cantons of the Swiss Confederation, the reform movement soon placed the Catholic areas of Switzerland on the defensive. As in Germany, civil war broke out between the cantons which embraced Zwinglianism and those which remained loyal to the old religion. After a brief but bloody conflict in which Zwingli lost his life, a truce was arranged in 1531, anticipating the same territorial toleration which characterized the German peace of 1555. Partly as a result of the stalemate, leadership in the Swiss Reformation passed from Zurich to the city of Geneva. There, at a moment crucial to the further progress of reform, appeared John Calvin, destined to become by far the most influential Protestant reformer.

## JOHN CALVIN AT GENEVA

CALVIN, born in northern France, was turned from his legal studies to the religious question first by the Catholic humanists, and then by the impact of Lutheran ideas upon a small group of French reformers. Embracing the cause of the Reformation, he fled to Switzerland when the French king, Francis I, scattered the Parisian Protestants.

No two men could have been more unlike than Luther and Calvin. In sharp contrast to Luther's warm-hearted emotional piety and explosive temperament, Calvin seems entirely devoid of sentiment in his stern and relentlessly logical approach to Christianity. But behind this cold exterior was a fanatical devotion to God's truth as he understood it, controlled and directed by an intellectual power that was equaled by few men in the sixteenth century. His learning was immense; his personal influence enormous. The *Institutes of the Christian Religion,* written when Calvin was only twenty-seven years old, presented Protes-

145

tantism with a complete and orderly system of doctrine, breathtaking in its scope and intensity. Within a few years it won Calvin the acclaim of all the reformed churches and remained for generations the basic theological textbook of Protestantism.

Calvin arrived at Geneva at the precise moment when the Reformation needed the strong hand of a vigorous organizer. Catholic authority had been repudiated in the city and the Mass already abolished, but reform was far from complete. The Swiss reformers in the various cantons were divided by dissension. Indeed, the entire Protestant cause was suffering from the inability of Lutherans and Zwinglians to reach theological agreement, especially concerning the nature of the sacraments and their place in the Christian life.

Moreover, radical groups flourished all through the countries that were in revolt against the papacy, alienating the sympathy which conservative reformers hoped to arouse among liberally minded Catholics. None of these was more detested than the Anabaptists, a fanatical sect of people who lived by the Bible as a book of law and strove to establish God's Kingdom among them upon earth. To both Catholics and Protestants the Anabaptist principles seemed to involve social revolution and the disruption of the civil order quite as much as dangerous religious aberrations. Zwingli drowned the Anabaptists at Zurich in horrible parody of their insistence upon adult baptism. Lutheran and Catholic troops fought side by side to free Münster from "the reign of the saints," a polygamous, communistic version of the Kingdom of God set up in that city by militant Anabaptist prophets.

Calvin proved to be exactly the man Protestantism needed. Within a decade or so he had reduced Geneva to his authority and that of his Consistory of Elders. Before a quarter-century had elapsed he had united the Swiss Protestants into what came to be known as the Reformed Church, and sent the dynamic influences of Genevan Calvinism into Scotland, Holland, France, England, and the Rhineland. Lutheranism remained Germanic and Scandinavian; Calvinism produced an international Reformed Church.

## CALVIN'S THEOLOGY

THE theological ideas of Calvin are often uncongenial to the modern mind. His insistent stress upon the awful majesty and righteousness of God drove him to emphasize with equal severity the utter worthlessness of fallen and sinful man. As Calvin understood the Holy Scriptures to which he, like Luther, appealed as the sole authority in matters of faith, the scheme of man's salvation involved belief in predestination. By the eternal decree of God's justice sinful man deserves nothing from a holy and righteous God. He is foreordained to damnation. But by the eternal power of God's mercy some men are chosen for salvation, not for their deserving, but solely because Christ has won them that mercy upon the cross.

The central point of this harsh doctrine of *election*, as it is called, is the belief that man's salvation rests entirely upon the merciful grace of Almighty God. However uncongenial might be the expression of this conviction in the form of a doctrine of predestination, the central truth still remains apart from any doctrine about it. No man can win eternal life by his own efforts. No man can storm the gates of heaven by the mere performance of external works of piety or formal religious observance. The response of man to God's outreaching grace that Luther tried to express in the idea of justification by faith, Calvin put in terms of predestination. Only by the infinite mercy that tempered God's unswerving justice could those fore-ordained to salvation be numbered among "the Elect in Jesus Christ."

The effects of this doctrine upon the religion of the ordinary man in the sixteenth century were revolutionary. It filled men with "sweet, pleasant, and unspeakable comfort." The followers of Calvin lived in the assurance that the spirit of Christ worked within them, drawing them ever more and more toward that perfection to which God had called them. Thus while on one hand Calvinism emphasized the utter worthlessness of the human creature, on the other it asserted the supreme dignity of that same worthless man when God in His mercy had chosen to number him among the elect. God's gracious mercy had placed a new value upon man, and that conviction strengthened the faith and increased the devotion of those who received this Gospel.

Nothing is more remarkable than the tremendous sense of personal responsibility aroused by the spirituality of Calvinism. It nurtured that sturdy, God-fearing moral character, marked by a high sense of personal integrity and unflinching courage, which is associated with Puritanism at its best. In the Reformed Church there was created a responsible, zealous, and well-informed laity who were often the chief agents of the extension of Calvinism throughout the western world. It is not surprising that in the sixteenth century this piety was combined with a spirit of legalism and a cruel intolerance. Religion was still man's first concern in the age of the Reformation, and its power rested upon the passionate allegiance of those for whom God's truth was literally a matter of life and death both here and hereafter.

## THE GENEVAN THEOCRACY

UNLIKE Luther, Calvin was deeply interested in the form and structure of the Visible Church upon earth. In that fellowship the sacraments were rightly administered; here the elect received the saving Word of God. Consequently, the ministry to whom the preaching of the Word and the governance of the Church was committed was of intense importance to the Calvinistic reformers.

Rejecting the Catholic hierarchy with its priestly ministry, Calvin returned to the Scriptures to reconstruct in his day a ministerial order similar to that which he found in the New Testament. Scripture was not only the sole authority in matters of faith; it contained, according to Calvin, explicit directions concerning Church order and organization. Out of Calvin's reconstruction came the presbyterian principle as accepted by the Reformed Churches. As he interpreted the ministry of the primitive Church, there were only two sorts of Church officers: the ordained presbyters, who might be either ministerial elders (pastors of the flock), or lay elders (rulers of the flock); and deacons, lay officers whose special charge was the care of the sick and the poor. Like Luther, Calvin rejected not only the papacy and the Catholic hierarchy, but also the ancient episcopal form of Church order that had been an integral part of the pattern of Christendom for fifteen hundred years.

Similarly, regarding all things as unlawful that were not expressly enjoined in Holy Scripture, the *Ecclesiastical Ordinances* of Geneva regulated public worship in minute detail. The evangelical services were of the simplest sort, consisting of Bible reading, psalm, and prayer, marked by frequent periods of religious instruction and constant preaching of the Word. Not only were the old externals of medieval ceremonial worship abandoned, but even the joy and beauty of religious art and music were ruthlessly suppressed.

As with public worship, so also the Consistory of Geneva dealt with public and private morals. Card playing and dancing were sins only slightly less reprehensible than drunkenness and fornication. Absence from sermon was punished as severely as addiction to popery. "Criticizing the ministers" or "defaming Calvin" were offenses that ranked with blasphemy. Calvinism had its ugly side in the blue laws that we associate with the later Puritanism of many of our New England ancestors.

Calvin's ideal was the theocratic state. In this there was little difference between the view of Calvinism and that of the medieval papacy. The civil authorities were expected to protect and support the Church, acting in its interests at the direction of the ministers.

In practice, the full achievement of this ideal varied from place to place, largely dependent upon local circumstances. In France, for example, the Reformed Church of the French Huguenots, always a minority with little chance of capturing the Catholic monarchy, struggled for freedom to regulate its life without interference from either civil or religious authorities. In Scotland, on the other hand, where the Calvinistic reformers swept Catholicism from the country, the domination of John Knox and his ministers was as complete as the medieval papal control had been at the height of its power. There are times in the history of those states to which Calvinism spread when we can readily understand the bitter comment of John Milton that this "new presbyter is but old priest writ large."

## REFORM IN ENGLAND

THE religious disturbances in Germany and Switzerland found a ready echo in England. The activity of the group of distinguished Catholic reformers had turned the minds of many earnest Englishmen to the urgent need for reform both in the Church's institutional life and in the abuses of everyday religious practice. Under the patronage of Archbishop Warham of Canterbury, the scholars of the New Learning were seeing the Scriptures in a new light. Theologians turned from the scholastic writings of the Middle Ages to explore again the ancient works of the Fathers of the Early Church. Thus influences from the Continental Reformation fell on increasingly fertile ground in England.

Lutheran ideas reached England largely through the contacts of the rising commercial and mercantile classes with the trading cities along the coasts of Germany and the Netherlands. Despite the vigilance of the ecclesiastical authorities, Lutheran books were smuggled into England in large numbers, passing from hand to hand among the ever-widening circle of clergy and laymen concerned with reform. Anabaptist and other radical influences followed in the trail of Lutheranism, fanning the smouldering remnants of England's medieval evangelicalism to a new outbreak of protest against the evils of the papal Church.

England in the early years of Henry VIII seethed with religious unrest. It was quite clear that in some form the Reformation would come to the country. The real question was "What course would it take?" As events proved, that course was unique among the Reformation experiences of the nations of Europe.

At the very outset the Reformation in England was not a religious revolution, but a political and constitutional crisis. It was precipitated, not by an uprising against the old religion but by a quarrel between the king of England and the Roman pope. The peculiar factors in the past history of the relations between England and the papacy widened this quarrel to make it one between the English nation and an alien power. Henry's original dispute with the pope was political, not religious, and through this quarrel there was suddenly projected into the explosive atmosphere of the sixteenth century all the accumulated friction between England's self-conscious nationality and the hostile, foreign interference of the papacy. Thus the separation of the Church in England from the foreign jurisdiction of the see of Rome, however much Henry VIII directed and controlled the forces involved, was an act with which virtually the whole nation identified itself. King and clergy, Parliament and people, all united in abolishing the papal power in the National Church.

## HENRY VIII AND THE PAPACY

THE immediate occasion of the repudiation of papal authority in England was the demand of the king for an annulment of his marriage to Katherine of Aragon. In 1509 England had hailed the accession of the talented and attractive Prince Henry with delight. All England's national self-consciousness was personified in this young Tudor monarch. He seemed the very embodiment of the dawning greatness of the English people in the western world.

But twenty years later the future of England's expanding political power and economic prosperity was in jeopardy. Henry VIII and Katherine had no male children. England was without a legitimate male heir to the throne. To a generation of men who saw the continued security and prosperity of the realm bound up with the peaceful accession of another Tudor prince, the situation was alarming. One of Katherine's children had lived, the Princess Mary. But that intensified rather than relieved the threat to the national security. Once only had a woman occupied the English throne—and that four hundred years before during a period of barbarous civil strife in which her title was bitterly contested. Could the Princess Mary succeed her father peaceably? Would not the surviving claimants of the Plantagenet royal family plunge England into dissension? And perhaps more dreaded by Englishmen in this nationalistic age, what if Mary married a foreign prince or monarch? Would not England then be brought under the domination of a European power?

We are easily led astray from this main issue to concentrate upon Henry's infatuation for Anne Boleyn, but the fact is that Anne was only the means to the real end: the provision of a prince to follow his father upon the throne. Under this pressure Henry VIII asked Pope Clement VII to annul his marriage with Katherine of Aragon. There was nothing uncommon in the request. Such annulments were frequent in the Renaissance age. Desperately anxious over the succession, Henry pressed his case ardently in 1527. A combination of circumstances, however, placed Henry's appeal in a special category among these royal matrimonial troubles.

The pope was at the moment virtually the prisoner of the Emperor Charles V, nephew of Katherine of Aragon. The papal political alliance against the imperial forces had gone awry, and Charles' troops occupied Rome. Clement was scarcely in a position to refuse to hear Katherine's appeal against Henry's proposal even had he been inclined so to do. Charles V would allow no move against his aunt. Furthermore, the situation was complicated by the fact that Katherine had been previously married to Henry's older brother Arthur, a prince who died in his youth. Twenty years before, in order that Henry might marry the young widow (a union which Henry VII considered politically desirable) Pope Julius II had issued a special dispensation. To the Medieval Church "in-law" relationships were as blood relationships. By this dispensation Julius II set aside the canon law which forbade marriage with sister-in-law or brother-in-law. Now Clement VII was asked to declare null and void a sentence given by his predecessor in the papal chair. It was an act that he feared would discredit further the papal authority which was already so drastically challenged in northern Europe.

CLEMENT delayed, unwilling to allow judgment to be given on Henry's demand and hoping that some fortunate circumstance might resolve the issue. Henry, at last convinced that the justice he felt was due him would not be forthcoming from Rome, shifted his attack to other grounds. Questions were raised that foreshadowed the end of papal power in England.

By what right did the pope deny justice to Henry's cause? Was this not still another example of the long tyranny the papacy had exercised over England's rightful independence? The answers already framed in their minds, Englishmen explored their own history for confirmation. The resistance of William I to the demands of the pope was cited in evidence of England's ancient freedom from foreign tyranny. The struggle between Henry II and Thomas Becket was seen to have contemporary significance. The parliamentary statutes in which medieval England had registered its protest against the extension of papal control over the English Church now appeared in a new light.

Still more telling were the doubts, conscientious or not, that were raised concerning Henry's marriage to Katherine in the first place. Did Pope Julius II have a right to allow such a union? How far did the pope have the power to set aside the canon law, especially when that law rested not upon a man-made regulation but upon the very Word of God itself? Was not the divine injunction of Holy Scripture clear in *Leviticus* 20:21: *And if a man shall take his brother's wife, it is an unclean thing. . . . they shall be childless.*

155

The procrastination of Clement VII was fatal to papal power in England. In 1529 Henry summoned what was destined to be the most important Parliament in English history. The attack upon the papacy began at once, and within four years a series of parliamentary statutes had extinguished papal authority in the English Church.

Appealing to "divers sundry old authentic histories and chronicles" in which the sovereign State of England was declared rightly free from both "the annoyance of the see of Rome as well as from the authority of other foreign potentates," Parliament turned the Church *in* England into the Church *of* England. The legislative assembly of the English Church (Convocation of the Clergy) solemnly declared that the Roman pontiff had no more authority in England than any other foreign bishop, and the orthodoxy of the National Church was proclaimed when Parliament assured the world that by none of its statutes was there any intention to "decline or vary from . . . the ancient Catholic faith of Christendom."

Henry secured his annulment when English bishops in convocation voted that no power upon earth could set aside the scriptural prohibition of marriage with a brother's widow. Thomas Cranmer, consecrated Archbishop of Canterbury just before the break with Rome, delivered judgment in his court in accordance with that episcopal decision.

### THE ENGLISH NATIONAL CHURCH

THE legislation of the Reformation Parliament declared the King's Majesty to be "the only Supreme Head in earth of the Church of England." It recognized the right of the crown "to visit, reform, correct, and restrain all such errors, heresies, and abuses which by spiritual authority or jurisdiction ought to be reformed and amended." This was the famous *Royal Supremacy* in the English Church of which so much has been written. No reformer thought this royal power to be other than an ancient prerogative rightfully possessed by the Christian monarch. "The Kings of Israel exercised it; so did the Roman emperors; so did the ancient Kings of England" wrote Stephen Gardiner, Bishop of Winchester and most staunchly conservative of Henry's ecclesiastics. "Surely I can see no reason," he continued, "why any man should be offended that the King is called the head of the Church of England rather than the head of the Realm of England, seeing that the Church of England consisteth of the same sort of people at this day that are comprised in this word Realm . . ."

Here is expressed the familiar medieval idea that Church and State were but two aspects of the same single undivided society. Royal supremacy was the English counterpart of the Lutheran doctrine of the sacred character of civil authority, and to men of the day it rested firmly on the tradition of the Bible. Nothing could be more unjust to Tudor Churchmen than the accusation that here is "the enslavement of the Church by the State." Such a concept assumes that by the *State* one means a purely secular power separate from and standing over against the *Church,* or purely religious society.

To the Tudors Church and State were inseparable names for the same single society. They lived in the last lingering sunset of the medieval ideal of the single Christian Commonwealth, now reduced to the national borders of England. Here the Christian prince stands at the head of the Christian nation. In his sacred office and responsibility he administers justice and maintains truth under God in spiritual as well as temporal causes. Here is the Christian State whose other name is Church. Here is the nation of one heart and mind, one loyalty and obedience in both faith and citizenship, the very embodiment of the scriptural principle of order in human society.

It is difficult for us to understand this point of view. We live in an age when religion is regarded as a purely private exercise, and when temporal authority is thought to be wholly secular in character. In a world where Church and State are apparently permanently sundered, it is hard to find meaning in the idea that the civil power is ordained of God and in some sense sacred. Yet in our time we are increasingly aware that no adequate doctrine of the Church can be formulated that does not relate to its redemptive mission the fact of nationality among men as well as the character of the modern state. The Tudor solution may be of little help to us, but it reminds us that in essence our problem is the same as theirs: *to make the Church the redemptive force in and of the national life.*


## NATIONAL CATHOLICISM IN ENGLAND

NOTHING could have been more unlike the revolutionary turmoil that seized Germany and Switzerland than the surprising ease and quietness with which Englishmen abandoned their allegiance to the papacy. To all outward appearances the Church functioned exactly as it had done before, the former jurisdiction of the pope being divided between the monarch and the Archbishop of Canterbury. The religious life of the ordinary man saw few changes.

The one violent act of Henry's religious settlement was the suppression of the convents and the monasteries. Here the king and his nobles were certainly motivated by a desire to lay hands upon much of the enormous wealth and property controlled by the monastic institution. Yet few voices were raised to halt this ruthless spoliation. The truth was that the invaluable contributions that the great monasteries had made to the cultural and economic life of the nation in the Middle Ages were now a thing of the far distant past. In the Reformation age the monasteries could justify their continued existence only by the extent and character of their influence in the religious life of the land. The significant point is that it was precisely in spiritual influence that the monastic institution had declined far from its original ideal. It was the growing spirit of secularism both within and without the monastic houses which engulfed them.

## REFORM UNDER AUTHORITY

With the disappearance of papal authority, the leaders of reform in the National Church undertook to eliminate the worst of the evils in the Church's faith and practice. Henry was persuaded to order the new English Bible to be set up in the churches that all his subjects might know "the very lively word of God, that every Christian man is bound to embrace, believe, and follow, if he look to be saved." Statements of traditional Catholic doctrine were issued upon the king's authority, purged of many of the superstitious interpretations placed upon these doctrines in the Middle Ages. The clergy were required to teach their people the Creed, the Ten Commandments, and the Lord's Prayer in English, as well as to give frequent instruction in the essentials of the Catholic faith. A determined effort was made to end the abuses surrounding the old practices of pilgrimage and excessive veneration of images. If all the corruptions in ordinary religious practice were not destroyed in Henry's reign, at least the forces were then set in motion which would one day see their disappearance.

There Henry VIII rested. As long as he lived the National Church would not move beyond the bounds of traditional orthodoxy. If Henry made overtures to the Protestant princes of Germany, it was with an eye to political alliance and not an attraction to the doctrines of the *Confession of Augsburg*. Henry might repudiate the papacy, but the English Church would remain loyal to Catholicism. The king had no intention of making a mockery out of a title once bestowed upon him by the pope in the years of his youth. Henry and his successors would continue to bear proudly the name "Defender of the Faith."

The abolition of the power of the pope in England came in the middle of Henry's reign. For two decades afterwards the English Church clung steadfastly to this National Catholicism. The effect of these twenty years of loyalty to the old tradition of faith and practice was to place the *principle of continuity* squarely in the center of what we now call Anglicanism. And there this emphasis on continuity with the past remained. Throughout the whole Reformation experience of the English Church the centrality of this principle controlled and directed those forces which made for doctrinal change and modification in religious life and practice. If the Reformation brought a new spirit into English religion, it brought it within the unchanged structure of the old Church. Such was the legacy of the National Catholicism of Henry VIII and his bishops.

## PROTESTANT EXPERIMENT AND CATHOLIC REACTION

WITH the death of Henry VIII in 1547, the English Reformation entered a new phase: six years of Protestant experiment in the reign of Edward VI, followed by six years of Catholic reaction under Mary I.

During the first half-dozen years the more zealous reformers, released from Henry's restraining hand, drew the Church closer to the patterns of Continental reform. With prominent Lutheran and Swiss reformers welcomed everywhere in England, and given influential posts in the universities, it seemed for a short space as though the end-product of the English Reformation might bear an unmistakably Swiss or German stamp.

This radical religious movement during the brief reign of Edward VI was largely stimulated and directed by the unscrupulous councillors of the young king. Bent upon personal acquisition of wealth and power, a small group of prosperous merchants and great landowners skillfully manipulated the forces of religious unrest to serve their own ends. Protecting and encouraging the activities of Protestant reformers in every step which would break the power of the Church, they transferred a large share of ecclesiastical wealth and property to their own pockets.

Subordinated to such control, the religious changes in these six years took place with bewildering rapidity.

The reign of Edward opened with a Parliament which repealed the heresy laws and recent penal statutes enforcing the old religion; made legal the marriage of the clergy; and ordered the provision of vernacular church services. Simultaneously, a set of royal injunctions, expanding those of the previous reign, attempted to destroy such "monuments of superstition" as still remained in the English Church. With some justice it may be maintained that these initial steps were designed to carry the program of reform begun under Henry VIII to its logical conclusion. But in the absence of any controlled plan of reform, and with the subordination of all religious change to the ambitions of the councillors, chaos and lawlessness were the inevitable result. Bishops interpreted the injunctions in their own fashion. Each advocate of reform became virtually a law unto himself. Before men's eyes the government set an example of supreme lawlessness, completely disregarding the statutory legislation and constitutional procedure which still existed to control and govern the life of the National Church.

By the end of the six years of Edward's reign, the Council was ruling England in both civil and ecclesiastical affairs with a tyranny that knew no check. The majority of the conservative bishops were deprived and imprisoned, men of Protestant conviction being intruded into their places. Churches were stripped of their valuable ornaments and possessions to enrich the powerful leaders of the government; the lords of the council systematically plundered the endowments of the dioceses. By 1553 nearly all the ancient external customs and observances of Catholicism had disappeared in England. In the very last months of Edward's life a set of forty-two doctrinal articles, markedly influenced by Continental confessions, was issued upon no greater authority than an arbitrary order of the Council.

The state-made reforms of Edward's government were far from popular, and the sudden death of the young king in 1553 revealed how little this Protestantism had penetrated the nation. Mary Tudor, the staunchly Catholic daughter of Henry VIII and Katherine of Aragon, succeeded to the throne amid an enthusiasm which swept nearly all England. But if the people hailed the end of an era of Protestant experiment with manifest joy, it was quite clear that the nation was not prepared to accompany the new queen to the limits of her reactionary program.

## ENGLAND UNDER MARY I

MARY'S first step was the repeal of all the religious acts of the previous reign, reviving the National Catholicism of her father. The next move, accomplished against considerable opposition in 1555, was the recognition of papal authority. All the ecclesiastical legislation of Henry VIII was withdrawn as Mary tried to put back the clock twenty-five years. England once again acknowledged the pope. But it was too late for Mary's efforts to be crowned with real success.

Half-Spanish, both in blood and in her own severe and intolerant piety, the queen had been for years isolated from the changing scene in England. She never understood the religious temper of the people whose ruler she became in 1553. Nothing, for example, could have been more disastrous to her hopes for a revival of loyalty to the papacy than her determination to check the course of the Reformation by condemning the reformers to death for heresy.

Against the wisest counsels of Mary's advisers, some three hundred Englishmen were burned at the stake as Protestant heretics. Among them were four bishops, including the Archbishop of Canterbury, Thomas Cranmer. Mary was determined to make examples of the leaders of reform; she succeeded in making them martyrs. It is small wonder that the queen enters history as "Bloody Mary," or that the name of Rome was feared and detested among Englishmen for generations. "Be of good comfort, Master Ridley," cried Bishop Latimer to his colleague as the two old men were dragged to the stake in Oxford, "we shall this day light such a candle by God's grace in England that shall never be put out!" It was a cry that echoed in Englishmen's memories for a long time.

The new obedience to Rome was scarcely more than a matter of form. Papal authority existed in name only. For three years England waited uneasily but patiently, all hopes centered upon the heir to the throne, the Princess Elizabeth. The last of Henry's children, she was known to be sympathetic to the Reformation. Englishmen waited abroad as well as at home. There, in the Protestant cities of Germany and Switzerland, those who had fled to the continent upon the accession of Mary Tudor kept alive the reformed religion as they had known it in the days of Edward VI. There also they came under the continental influences that were to play such a large part in the Elizabethan settlement of religion when the exiles returned to England.

THE central figure in these two brief reigns which inter-vene between those of Henry VIII and Elizabeth is Arch-bishop Cranmer. Few men have left such a deep mark upon Anglicanism as this gentle, conscientious scholar on whose shoulders the burden of leadership in the English Reformation fell when Henry died in 1547. The Anglican tradition owes much to his tolerant forbearance and sym-pathetic understanding of other opinions than his own. It owes perhaps still more to that final struggle of heart and mind in which Thomas Cranmer, faced with death at the stake, sought to find the answer to the ultimate question raised by the Reformation: Where does final authority in Christianity lie? Where is the truth of the living God made known to men?

Steeped in the New Learning since his student days at Cambridge, Cranmer had long been the earnest opponent of papal authority in England. Like the reformers else-where in Europe, he was convinced that the claim of the pope to supremacy over all Christendom had no warrant either in Holy Scripture or in the history of the ancient Church. Brought to the notice of Henry VIII largely be-cause of this conviction, the king prevailed upon the pope to authorize the consecration of Cranmer as archbishop on the eve of the break with Rome. Thus for twenty-three crucial years Thomas Cranmer found himself in what was at once the post of greatest opportunity and greatest re-sponsibility in the Church of England.

Essentially a scholar, Cranmer was a man temperamen-tally more at home in the quiet quadrangles of a university than in the turbulent court of a Tudor monarch. Deeply disturbed by the erroneous doctrines and superstitious practices that were allowed to distort the religion of the ordinary man in the Medieval Church, Cranmer's first concern was with reform in the Church's worship. He saw the masses of his countrymen denied participation in the great corporate act of worship in the Holy Communion by the insuperable barrier of the Latin language. The evangelizing power of the Lord's own service could not reach them.

With acute spiritual perception Cranmer realized that nothing was more important to the cause of true religion than liturgical reform. Men might issue injunctions, legislate reforms with new authority, or publish innumerable statements concerning doctrine. These would be vain unless men could lay hold upon the living truth where they came in closest touch with God—in prayer and sacrament. Thus Cranmer's long-cherished project was the reform of the services of the Church of England. More than any other individual, he is responsible for what became the finest possession of Anglicanism, *The Book of Common Prayer*.

Conservative in all matters save those of the recognition of the pope and the most glaring abuses in church life, Henry VIII refused to allow his archbishop a free hand in revising the Church's services. It was Cranmer who succeeded in persuading the king to require the parish clergy to teach their people the Lord's Prayer, the Creed, and the Ten Commandments in English, and to order the new English Bible to be set up in the churches. Further than that Henry could not be pushed, with one notable exception. In 1544 he yielded to Cranmer's urging and allowed the archbishop to issue the magnificent English litany which was later incorporated into the Anglican Prayer Book. Translated partly from sections of Latin litanies in use in the Medieval Church, and partly from a Lutheran litany, it displays Cranmer's deep spiritual perception, as well as his masterly skill in the use of the English language.

## THE BOOK OF COMMON PRAYER

WITH the death of Henry VIII in 1547 the work of liturgical reform proceeded more rapidly. Edward's councillors, bent upon their own attack upon the Church's power and property, gave the archbishop a free reign in purely religious reform. Steps were taken at once toward a vernacular liturgy. The Bible lessons of Matins and Vespers (the morning and evening services of the Church), as well as the Creed, Epistle, and Gospel at Mass were read in the language of the people. When Edward's Parliament, returning to the ancient customs of the Church, enacted that henceforth the people should receive at communion the Chalice as well as the sacred Host, Cranmer had ready for publication in 1548 a simple *Order for the Communion* of the people. Designed to encourage frequent communions as well as providing forms for the reception of the Sacrament in both kinds, this Order consisted of English devotions to be used in conjunction with the Latin Mass.

In 1549 Cranmer's work in liturgical revision came to fulfilment. On Whitsunday of that year the revised and translated services were published in the new *Book of Common Prayer,* ordered for use throughout the realm.

Here in *The Book of Common Prayer* the principles that guided the archbishop in his reform of the liturgy are quite clear.

Apart from the task of purging the ancient services of accumulations of erroneous doctrine and superstitious practice, the simplification of the complexity of the old service books was one of Cranmer's chief aims. The array of liturgical books necessary to the worship of the Medieval Church was reduced to one convenient volume. Between its covers were bound the revised and translated services formerly in the *Breviary,* the *Missal,* and the *Manual.* Here, in one uniform use for the whole English Church, the devotional heritage of a thousand years of Christianity was given to the people in their own tongue.

Simplification and convenience, uniformity, the vernacular language—these were not the only aims of Thomas Cranmer. He was concerned also to restore to the Church's worship the scriptural character that it had anciently possessed. Over the years of the Middle Ages the biblical foundation of the Church services had ceased to be plain. Evangelical doctrines had become obscured; readings from Holy Scripture had been replaced by "uncertain stories and legends." The restoration of the language and the ideas of the Bible to the people's worship was one of the significant accomplishments of *The Book of Common Prayer.* The religion of the new Prayer Book was the religion of the Bible. And it is this scriptural character of Anglican services that largely accounts for the power of the Prayer Book in the minds and hearts of men for the past four hundred years.

## THE PRAYER BOOK CONTROVERSY

IN THE disturbed condition of England during the last years of Edward VI's reign, few people were satisfied with the new English services. Conservative clergy were uneasy with what seemed to be innovations in worship. Radical reformers, from whom the chief opposition to the Prayer Book came, felt that the services were patterned far too closely after the traditional forms of worship in the Medieval Church. As a result of violent controversy, Cranmer made some drastic modifications in the Prayer Book of 1549, mostly in the direction of further simplicity and greater emphasis upon the evangelical doctrines of the Reformation.

The Holy Communion service, for example, was reduced to its bare essentials. All the ancient psalms, salutations, and other devotional enrichments were eliminated. Prayers for the dead, and other forms of devotion which might lend themselves to superstitious interpretations along the lines of the old religion, were omitted. Even the sentence with which the Sacrament was administered to the people was altered. *Take and eat this in remembrance* . . . was substituted for the ancient form *The body of our Lord Jesus Christ which was given for thee* . . . for fear that men who heard the old words might be beguiled into some Romish superstition concerning the sacred elements. In addition to these changes, the various prayers of the Communion Office were arbitrarily rearranged so that the resulting service appeared to bear little resemblance to the medieval Mass. With such revision the Prayer Book was published again in 1552, but it had scarcely come into use before the untimely death of Edward VI altered the entire situation. Upon the accession of Mary Tudor the Latin services were again resumed. All Cranmer's work had apparently come to naught.

## THE DEATH OF CRANMER

WITH the arrest of the leading reformers, Queen Mary was determined that Cranmer should suffer the extreme penalty for leading England into heresy. In her view he was the archtraitor, false to his oath to the pope, the betrayer of the souls of his countrymen. She was convinced that the sight of the archbishop making abject submission and recanting his heresies would discredit the Reformation forever in the eyes of Englishmen.

As Cranmer lay in prison during the long months while the papal court was occupied with his condemnation and sentence, he wrestled with a cruel dilemma. His whole religious position had been founded upon an appeal away from the authority of the pope to the independence of a National Church free from all foreign interference. The royal supremacy of a Christian prince had been the keystone in his concept of authority in religion. Now that principle was a broken reed in his hand. Mary, to whom he owed the obedience in spiritual matters due a Christian monarch, was returning England to the ungodly yoke of the papacy by the exercise of the very royal supremacy itself. Where could his appeal against Rome rest now? What was his conscientious duty?

It was this bitter internal struggle in the last few weeks of his life that prompted Cranmer's recantations and changes of mind. Uncertain almost to the end, it was not until the final hours before his death that the path of duty became clear in his mind. He at last declared himself against pope and queen alike. Repudiating a royal supremacy which would bind England once more to the papal tyranny and the doctrines of Romanism, Cranmer died for the supremacy of the Christian conscience over all external authority.

In that final scene in Oxford in 1555 when the archbishop stood among the flames, there was forged into the core of Reformation Anglicanism still another strand which would bind men to God's truth: the authority of the living voice of God speaking through the thought and spiritual experience of each generation. Already in emerging Anglicanism the Catholic authority of historic continuity or the tradition of the Church had been subjected to the correcting and revitalizing influence of the Evangelical authority of Scripture. Now a third element fuses these two in the creative center of the ethos of Anglicanism. Henceforward the Church of England will regard both tradition and Scripture as interpreted by the constant operation of the Holy Spirit in the Christian Fellowship, linking men to that continuous stream of the Church's life and experience which is the tradition, and illuminating their understanding of the eternal character of the Word of God.

## THE ELIZABETHAN SETTLEMENT

In 1558 the Reformation in England entered its final constructive phase, the character of which was largely determined by the events of the two preceding decades. Queen Elizabeth was the child of the Renaissance in more ways than one. Combining the political astuteness of Machiavelli with the humanism of Erasmus, the queen kept a sensitive finger upon the spiritual pulse of her people. She took for her starting-point the religious settlement of her father. The anti-papal legislation of Henry VIII again became the constitutional basis of the English Church. To this Elizabeth added those religious acts of Edward VI that had brought the reforms of Henry to their natural conclusion. Royal supremacy was thus restored, but with some significant modifications. The queen had the good sense to learn, both from the abuse of power by her father and the era of unrestrained experiment in the reign of her half-brother.

Elizabeth abandoned the earlier bald and unqualified assertion of the power of the crown over the Church. No longer did the statement read "The Supreme Head of the Church of England in earth, next under Christ, is the King of England." Now more guarded phrases declared that "the Queen's Highness is the only supreme governor of this realm." This governorship was discussed at length and with disarming frankness in the *Injunctions of 1559* and in the later *Thirty-Nine Articles*. It was, claimed Elizabeth, "only that prerogative which we see to have been given always to all godly Princes in Holy Scripture by God Himself—that is, that they should rule all estates and degrees committed to their charge, whether they be Ecclesiastical or Temporal."

The practice of the queen made the limitations of royal supremacy even clearer. Henry wielded his ecclesiastical authority with no check upon his personal whim; Elizabeth kept herself strictly within the provisions of the religious legislation, exercising the royal power in the

Church through the representative commission of Churchmen that was provided by the statutes. Protected rather than oppressed by the crown, the Elizabethan Church enjoyed freedom from all other interference. Parliament was not permitted to meddle in matters ecclesiastical, Elizabeth stoutly maintaining that the governance of the Church was the proper sphere of Convocation and her bishops. To this principle she adhered rigidly throughout her long reign, frustrating repeated attempts of Puritan Parliaments to alter the structure or interfere with the life of the English Church. Royal supremacy was not parliamentary supremacy.

In principle, Elizabeth's settlement remains the constitutional basis of the English Church. Forty years after her death the momentary triumph of Puritanism, in the rebellion of Parliament against the absolutism of Charles I, temporarily dissolved the Anglican establishment and plunged England into religious chaos. But with the return of the Stuart monarchy in 1660, the Elizabethan settlement again became the basis of the established Church. Today, despite repeated modification, it is still the underlying constitutional foundation of the Church of England.

### THE POLICY OF CONCILIATION

THE chief aim of Elizabeth's careful definition of her supremacy was the conciliation of the Catholics. She required of her subjects little more than assent to the religious implications of a nationalist political theory. Within the limits of that theory the Church was free to lead its own life. If Englishmen would give outward conformity to their Church, the queen would not make men's consciences bear any greater strain than necessary to the security of the realm. Catholics might believe as they would, provided they conformed. As Elizabeth put it "We will make no window into men's souls . . . our subjects shall not be molested for matters of faith as long as they show themselves conformable."

Conciliation was the central pivot of Elizabeth's whole ecclesiastical policy. With the national unity gravely imperiled by the religious strife of the two preceding reigns, the queen determined to win the loyalty of all her subjects to a comprehensive Church within the wide limits of which they could find religious unity. Every effort was made to make the settlement broad enough to include all but the most uncompromising Puritan or most obdurate papist. Along such lines the *Thirty-Nine Articles,* a series of statements concerning the particularly controversial doctrines of the sixteenth century, were framed. The *Articles* maintained the traditional Catholic element in the faith of the Church of England, while at the same time indicating the points of kinship with the Protestant Reformation.

Similarly, Elizabeth sought to make the 1552 Prayer Book more acceptable to her Catholic subjects. The petition in the litany against *the tyranny of the Bishop of Rome and all his detestable enormities* was quietly dropped. The so-called black rubric which forbade the adoration of the sacred elements and denied any real and essential presence of Christ's body and blood therein, was removed from the Communion service. The sentence of administration from the 1549 Prayer Book, *The body of our Lord Jesus Christ which was given for thee,* was restored, joined with the *Take and eat this in remembrance* of Edward VI's second book. Thus Elizabeth attempted to win the loyalty of Catholics in their deepest devotional experience, that of the Holy Communion. She would allow her subjects to believe, as she once expressed it herself:

> *Christ was the word that spake it,*
> *He took the bread and brake it;*
> *And what His words did make it*
> *That I believe and take it.*

With scrupulous care Elizabeth and her advisers made certain that the continuity of the Church of England was ensured by an unbroken line of bishops in the apostolic succession. Though nearly all Mary's Romanist bishops refused the oath of loyalty, the queen found a sufficient number of men in episcopal orders, consecrated under Henry VIII and Edward VI, to make Matthew Parker Archbishop of Canterbury in 1559.

The choice of Parker was a happy one. A distinguished scholar and historian, he realized that the appeal of Anglicanism against Rome was an appeal to Scripture and history. This he set out to demonstrate by collecting ancient chronicles and histories by which it could be proved that England in her Reformation had only sloughed off the popish innovations of the Middle Ages and returned to the faith and practice of the primitive Catholic Church. Parker's historical studies provided the ammunition for the magnificent defense of the Church of England against the Roman claims, undertaken by his friend Bishop Jewel of Salisbury, and entitled *Apologia Ecclesiae Anglicanae*. For generations the *Apologia* remained the classic expression of the claim of Anglicanism to continuity with the undivided Church in the first six centuries of her life.

## ELIZABETH AND THE ROMANISTS

WHILE scholars were thus vindicating Canterbury against Rome, the government was surprisingly tolerant in its attitude toward individual Roman Catholics. The vast majority of Englishmen conformed to the Elizabethan Church. Those who refused, or who nurtured conscientious scruples, received the secret ministrations of a small number of Marian clergy who had fled into hiding. But as long as Catholic Europe took no action against England the government could afford to be tolerant. The remnant of English Romanism, it seemed, would die a natural death with the eventual disappearance of the decreasing number of these secret "massing priests."

In 1570 the situation was radically altered. Pope Pius V, sternly forbidding attendance at the "damnable communion" of the Church of England, launched a papal judgment upon Queen Elizabeth. Excommunicating her for heresy, the pope declared the "pretended Queen" no longer the rightful ruler of England, and absolved her subjects from their political allegiance. English Roman Catholics were placed in an intolerable position. With the pope commanding Englishmen "that they presume not to obey [the queen] or her orders, mandates, and laws" on the pain of excommunication, the scrupulous Catholic might find treason to be his religious duty. Henceforth the government was forced to regard loyal Romanists as potential traitors. The answer to the pope's action was the series of anti-Romanist statutes that placed Roman Catholics in England under severe civil disabilities for nearly three hundred years.

The tension was further aggravated by the flight to England of the Catholic Mary Stuart of Scotland, Elizabeth's cousin and heir. Perpetually alarmed by Romanist plots to place Mary on the throne with the help of the Catholic powers abroad, Elizabethan England knew no relief from fear until the death of Mary and the defeat of the Spanish Armada.

From 1570 onwards Englishmen were increasingly aware that the papacy they now confronted was not the decadent Renaissance papacy which Henry VIII had known forty years before. A revival and reinvigoration had almost completely changed the character of the Roman Church. Testimony to the new Romanism was borne by the scores of devoted missionary priests and Jesuits who poured into England in the last quarter of the sixteenth century. Chiefly Englishmen trained in the new missionary colleges abroad, it is due to the heroic and perilous labors of these papal missionaries that a thin stream of native English Romanism survived the Reformation.

## THE ROMAN CATHOLIC REVIVAL ON THE CONTINENT

CLEMENT VII, the antagonist of Henry VIII and the last of the Renaissance popes, died in 1534. His successors formed a line of popes of completely different spirit and outlook. Rome was at last roused to control and direct the movement for Catholic reform. Too late to prevent the fragmentation of Christendom, the papacy nevertheless summoned all its resources to challenge the spread of Protestantism.

The activity of Roman Catholicism in the seventy-five years after 1534 is often known as the *Counter-Reformation,* a term which suggests the vigorous effort made by Roman Catholic forces to recover Europe to the papal obedience. But the Counter-Reformation was not limited to warfare with the Protestants, however relentlessly that battle was continued. There was at the same time a spontaneous spiritual reinvigoration within papal Catholicism which had, in the long run, significant effects upon the character of the Roman Church. Under the whole impact of this revival the old medieval Catholicism assumed the guise of modern Romanism.

## COUNTER-REFORMATION ACTIVITY

DISPLAYING remarkable singleness of purpose, the popes of the Counter-Reformation put aside the secular concerns and political ambitions that had dominated the papacy for generations. Self-interest gave place to an awakened sense of leadership in the crucial affairs of the Church, and all the vast resources at Rome's command were devoted to the recovery of the spiritual power of Catholic Christendom. Sweeping reforms freed the papal court and the Church at large of many of the accumulated abuses and corruptions. The formation of an official *Index* of prohibited books protected the faithful from heretical writings, while the simultaneous establishment of seminaries and missionary colleges prepared the Roman clergy to teach the old faith with new zeal and intelligence.

The *Inquisition,* which had operated intermittently and often with comparatively little efficiency in the Middle Ages, was reorganized under direct papal control. It speedily became one of the most efficient instruments of terror and repression which Europe has ever known, hunting down heresy and ecclesiastical rebellion everywhere that a Catholic government supported its operation. Rome was unstinting in her aid to such Catholic sovereigns as Philip II of Spain or the French Valois monarchs in their efforts to suppress the activity of their Protestant subjects. Conversely, Romanist subjects of Protestant princes were incited to rebellion and, it is alleged, in some cases, to the actual assassination of their rulers.

Behind this external activity of counter reform, there was the deeper spiritual revival of the Catholic West, a movement that began about the time Luther raised the standard of revolt in Germany. Originating in groups of serious-minded clergy and laymen who were concerned both with doctrinal reform and with inspiring a greater spirit of consecration among priests and people, the revival quickly spread throughout the Church. Signs of a real religious awakening were seen everywhere.

A new disciplined piety found expression in the wide influence of men like St. Charles Borromeo and St. Philip Neri; Catholic mysticism reached new heights of spiritual perception in St. Teresa of Avila and St. John-of-the-Cross. The intensity of the Counter-Reformation spirit was clearly revealed in its impact upon education, missionary activity, and works of mercy and charity. While in the sixteenth century the awakening reached its peak in Italy and Spain, it was still vigorous a hundred years later in France. There its strength is seen in the earnest efforts of St. Francois de Sales to convert the Protestants of Savoy and to raise the level of Catholic spirituality, and in the passionate concern of St. Vincent de Paul with the lot of the sick, the poor, and the underprivileged masses.

## THE NEW RELIGIOUS ORDERS

A NUMBER of religious orders sprang into being with this revival. Some, like the Carmelites and the Capuchins, were the result of the reconstitution of older medieval orders. Others, like the Ursulines, the Order of the Visitation, and the Sisters of Charity, were entirely new foundations, their rules implementing their work of charity, education, and evangelism. Among all these religious orders, the most famous was the Society of Jesus, the *Jesuits* of Ignatius Loyola. Founded in 1534 by a young Spaniard who turned from a soldier's career to a militant vocation in the Church, the Jesuits formed a disciplined army of men under vows of complete obedience, ready to serve the pope wherever he might send them. Their influence was enormous in every sphere of Counter-Reformation activity.

It was the Jesuits who soon controlled the new Roman Catholic educational system. Their teachers raised the level of seminary education for the clergy; their scholars dominated the Roman theological world. It was the Jesuits who spearheaded the advance of papal missionaries into Protestant countries to recover men to their allegiance to Rome. It was the Jesuits who appeared on the new missionary fronts of the world in the wake of the exploration of America and the Far East by the Roman Catholic nations of Europe. St. Francis Xavier followed the Portuguese to India, and from there beat a path that Roman

Catholic missionaries would follow to China and Japan. Other Jesuits accompanied the Spanish to South America and the French to Canada and the Mississippi valley. As long as the Jesuits retained the purity of their first ideals, the selfless and zealous heroism of the followers of Ignatius Loyola made them the chief agents of Roman Catholic recovery in Europe, and inscribed their names forever in some of the brightest missionary chapters in the history of Christianity.

## THE COUNCIL OF TRENT

THE spirit of reform and recovery that marked the Counter-Reformation found its concrete and permanent expression in the Council of Trent, the sessions of which occupied the mind of Roman Christendom from 1545 to 1563. Here in the decrees and canons of a council representing the world of papal obedience, the principles of this Roman Catholic revival were given dogmatic and authoritative form. In a very real sense the modern Roman Church dates from the sessions of the Council of Trent.

The most interesting decrees of Trent are those that give dogmatic expression to Christian doctrines in which considerable latitude of interpretation had been allowed in the Middle Ages. Henceforth in Romanism this systematic definition imposed a strict unity of belief. Modern Rome breathes an atmosphere of dogmatic rigidity that was unknown to Catholic Europe before this council. Likewise, the disciplinary canons, useful as they were in achieving reforms, fixed upon the new Romanism a narrowness of temper that was foreign to much of the older spirit of Catholicism.

## DOCTRINES OF THE NEW ROMANISM

AT THE Council of Trent Rome gave her official answer to that problem of authority in religion which vexed the sixteenth century. According to the Tridentine decrees, there are two equal sources of Christian truth, the Holy Scriptures and the tradition of the Church, but the two are related to each other in such a way that Scripture becomes little more than the written portion of the tradition. The statement of the Tridentine Council was clear: "All saving truth and discipline are contained in written books and unwritten traditions, which were received by the Apostles from the lips of Christ Himself, or by the same Apostles, at the dictation of the Holy Spirit, and were handed on and have come down to us . . ."

Little was said at Trent of the powers of the pope or the relation of the papal institution to the Church. "Holy Mother the Church" was the true judge and interpreter of the sense of Holy Scripture and, obviously, of the tradition. But the procedure of the council made it plain that the papacy was the one agency by which the mind of the Church on matters of faith and morals was to be declared. The doctrinal decrees of Trent were not valid until the papal publication of them; the disciplinary canons were accompanied by the qualifications ". . . saving in all things the authority of the Apostolic See." This procedure received confirmation in 1564 when Pope Pius IV published the decisions of the council, imposing upon all Roman clergy and others with teaching responsibility a *Profession of Faith* in which they gave unqualified allegiance to Tridentine Romanism.

Papal supremacy was assumed rather than defined at

the Council of Trent. Implicit in this assumption was a concept of supremacy which made the papacy the guardian and interpreter of all Christian truth necessary for salvation. It is not surprising to find that the next logical step from such supremacy was the definition of papal infallibility. By erecting within the Church an authoritative institution through which true Christian doctrine and right Christian behavior is made known, Roman Christendom found it an intellectual and moral necessity that such an institution be clothed with infallibility. Thus the Council of Trent led directly to the Vatican Council of 1870 where the character of papal supremacy was carefully defined. There the infallibility of the pope in declaring the mind of the Church on matters of faith and morals was made an essential article of modern Roman Catholic belief.

### THE WARS OF RELIGION

THE end of the Reformation era in Europe was marked by the terrible wars of religion which terminated the religious conflicts of the sixteenth and seventeenth centuries. Dominated by the belief that only one form of Christianity could be tolerated within the borders of the new national states, men everywhere turned to civil war as the final means of enforcing their religious convictions upon their neighbors. In the Netherlands the Dutch Calvinists and the Catholic Flemings fought bitterly until the separation of the Low Countries into Protestant Holland and Romanist Belgium isolated them from each other. In Germany and central Europe the Thirty-Years' War brought in its train such devastation as was unknown until the world wars of the twentieth century. In France the Catholics and the Protestant Huguenots massacred and murdered each other with unbelievable ferocity for nearly a half-century.

While all over Europe these conflicts were inseparable from nationalist struggles for political independence or economic expansion, they were at the outset wars of religion, undertaken primarily in the interests of Christian truth as men understood it. If motives of national security and prosperity were involved, it was because men were still convinced that unity in religion was vital to that security and prosperity. Terrible as these wars were, they bore testimony to the fact that religion was still the most important factor in man's life. Ideas, and in this case, religious ideas, were the most potent forces in the world.

A century later the successors of the men of the Reformation, indifferent to the vitality of the forces of religion, never understood their embattled Protestant and Catholic ancestors. But in our time we have come to understand again the power of ideas in its full potency. Conflicts that are basically ideological already have unleashed two ghastly world wars. It is increasingly clear that the quarrels which still threaten the peace of mankind spring from opposing concepts of the nature and destiny of man, the kind of a being he is, and his place in society; that is to say, essentially *religious* ideas.

### THE PURITAN REVOLT IN ENGLAND

IN ENGLAND the wars of religion took the form of a Puritan revolt against the established Anglican Church. Those least satisfied with the Elizabethan settlement were the zealous Protestant reformers. Having absorbed the spirit

184

of Calvinism in the days of their exile under Mary Tudor, or subsequently, they were determined to reproduce in England a Reformed Church on the Geneva model. For twenty years Elizabeth and her bishops fought the Puritan efforts to discard the Prayer Book in favor of a Protestant service book, to eliminate the elements of Catholicism from the religious life of Englishmen, and to alter the entire structure of the established Church by substituting for its episcopal order and government a presbyterian system and discipline similar to what the Puritans saw on the Continent and in Scotland.

Earnest and sincere reformers, the Elizabethan Puritans put their finger accurately upon many of the evils in the Anglican Reformation settlement. Continuity with the Medieval Church was all too clear in some respects. Standards of clerical education were low. The old abuses of holding benefices in plurality and the non-residence of rectors were still common. All the cumbersome machinery of the ecclesiastical courts, slow of justice and exorbitant of cost, still touched people at numerous points in everyday life.

The Elizabethan bishop seemed to the Puritans to bear little resemblance to a minister of God. While no longer a feudal baron, yet the apostolic character of the episcopal office was difficult to perceive in a prelate whose chief activity was that of an administrative servant of the crown. It can readily be understood why the Puritan leaders counted so many supporters among earnest lay folk. They seemed to be pleading the cause of true religion in which the things of God would be separated from the things of Caesar. But the Calvinist system is liable to its own particular abuses, as the events of the next century revealed to Englishmen. Had the revolt under Elizabeth been successful, Puritan intolerance would have imposed a religious system as unpalatable to the mass of the people as Anglicanism was to the few.

## THE INFLUENCE OF PURITANISM

THOUGH suppressed, largely through the opposition of the queen and Archbishop Whitgift, yet Puritanism had two notable results in Elizabeth's reign. First, it called forth the famous defense of the Church of England against Geneva, *The Laws of Ecclesiastical Polity* by Richard Hooker, the most notable Anglican scholar of the sixteenth century. Precisely as earlier John Jewel in his *Apologia* had appealed to Scripture and history to justify Anglicanism against Rome, so Hooker made a similar learned and temperate appeal to vindicate the Church of England against Puritanism.

The second result was perhaps more significant. Something of the passionate evangelical spirit of the Puritans was absorbed by the ecclesiastical establishment they sought to overthrow. Anglicanism, in the last of its formative years, was flexible enough to receive the impress of that which was of permanent value in the witness of Puritanism. The principle of continuity, established in the first years of the English Reformation, had placed a high value upon the historic Catholic elements in Anglicanism. Now to that reverence for unbroken continuity in faith and order, the corrective and inspiring influence of an evangelical emphasis was firmly joined.

Tension was inevitable when these two emphases were

brought together, but it was a tension that made possible a deeper understanding of the wholeness of God's truth in His Church. The evangelical concern with "Gospel before Church" would enable Anglicanism to call itself into judgment. The Catholic element, on the other hand, would bind the Church, even while under judgment, to the traditional stream of Christian life and experience in all ages. By means of this creative tension Anglicanism has remained aware that in a religion of Incarnation, history is both the means of God's self-revelation and the scene of God's redemption.

The full force of the wars of religion in England was released when Puritanism, driven underground by Elizabeth, reappeared under her Stuart successors. Allied with Parliamentary hostility to the absolutism of Charles I, Puritanism had its moment of victory during the Great Rebellion. Crown and Church were alike plucked down when King Charles and Archbishop Laud died upon the Puritan scaffold for the divine right of kings and for the Anglican establishment which the peculiar circumstances of the English Reformation had inseparably connected with the monarch. But as Church and Crown fell together, so they returned together. When the restoration of Charles II in 1660 brought an end to Cromwell's Commonwealth, the Anglican Church again became the religious establishment of the realm.

The seventeenth century left an abiding mark upon English religious life. Though perhaps not clear in 1660, it is apparent to us now that significant changes had occurred. The Tudor ideal of the nation with a single religious loyalty vanished when dissent from the Church of England came to be a permanent factor in English life. British citizenship was no longer coterminous with Anglican churchmanship. In one sense this freed the Church of England from the narrow channels of the Reformation concept of a National Church to seek its destiny as a free Catholic Church. Moreover, no longer was Anglicanism inseparably bound to the English monarchy. Royal supremacy would survive into the modern world only as the antiquarian peculiarity of one member of the worldwide family of Churches that make up the Anglican Communion.

## THE END OF THE REFORMATION AGE

GRADUALLY throughout Europe the wars of religion ceased. In the exhaustion that followed the long strife, what men have called the Age of Toleration dawned. Religious toleration has been hailed as one of the great moral advances of mankind in modern times, and so the Christian properly regards such toleration when it springs from religious motives and convictions. The toleration of the Gospel is the expression of Christian love for all the children of God, not indifference to all human opinions about God and mankind.

As we look back into the seventeenth century now, however, it is clear that men ceased to fight over their faith, not so much because they saw that the sword was not the weapon of Christianity, as because they came to believe that religion was not worth the battle. The enlightenment of the late seventeenth and eighteenth centuries bred toleration, but it was too often the toleration which springs from secular motives and aims. The wars of religion began in the universal conviction that faith was the most important factor in the lives of men and nations. These same wars ended in the belief that it was not worth endangering man's material welfare and economic prosperity for the sake of religion.

Few men in the seventeenth century perceived the essentially secular motivation of their tolerant spirit. We see it differently from the vantage point of the twentieth century when secularism has achieved its disastrous triumph. Yet the trend was clear at the end of the Reformation age. The events that ended the wars of religion in France, for example, are singularly instructive, perhaps because the French have always been remarkably unsentimental and realistic. Peace was brought about between Catholics and Huguenots in France by the *Edict of Nantes* in 1598. Engineered by men who saw France's security and prosperity endangered by the devastating religious strife, this truce allowed liberty of worship and full civic rights to French Protestants, while Catholicism remained the religion of the majority. Here was toleration springing not so much from Christian conviction as from concern for the welfare of society. A breach was made between religious uniformity and national life. Soon its character changed; it became a breach between religion and life. As the years went on, men sought to maintain Christian standards and social ideals, but with increasing disregard for the faith in which they were rooted. It was forgotten that the character of man's common life rests upon the faith that is in the hearts of the people.

Thus here in the beginnings of modern history the evil side of Renaissance humanism triumphed. The forces of secularism, against which in one sense the whole Reformation was a protest, were at last victorious in man's external world. The things of God were not only separated from those of Caesar, but ultimately regarded as totally irrelevant to them. All man's corporate activities, political and economic, social and intellectual, moved along the path that would divorce them from religion.

The ultimate tragedy of secularism is the unreality of it all. The truth is that there are no things of Caesar apart from God. This, at least, the men of the Reformation age knew. The slow and painful rediscovery of this truth in our time is the brightest gleam of hope for the world of tomorrow.

# CHAPTER FIVE

# Christianity in the
# Modern World

A BRIEF survey of the life of the Christian Church since the Reformation is bound to be topical and highly selective. Moreover, the divided aspect of modern Christendom imposes a somewhat disconnected pattern upon our treatment. From the wealth of material in modern Church history, space allows the selection of only the more significant events and movements.

The forces of secularism emerged victorious throughout a large part of the western world at the end of the wars of religion. The completeness of that victory was not apparent at once. Indeed, it did not become obvious in its most devastating form until it was manifested in the rejection of Christianity and the denial of the true nature of man by the contemporary totalitarian ideologies. Even today it is likely that we have not yet witnessed the full power of secularist ideals, but what we have seen in the past three centuries, and so often forgotten to notice, is the amazing vitality of Christianity in conflict with these forces that would tame, insulate, or eradicate men's faith in Christ.

## THE BEGINNINGS OF THE MODERN WORLD

IN SEEKING for one expression which would summarize briefly the basic difference between the medieval and the modern world, it has been said that in the Middle Ages men found ultimate meaning in life in terms of human community. In the Renaissance, and increasingly from then onwards in the modern era, men rejected the principle of community for that of individualism. There is a large measure of truth in this assertion. The medieval European world was one of community. Politically, the single Empire was the tangible manifestation of the one world to which men belonged. Socially and economically, the feudal system and the later guild and craft organizations accentuated the interlocking responsibilities and obligations binding men together in a single order. Undergirding this synthesis was the supreme membership of all in a Church that, related to men's lives at every point, constantly asserted the primacy of God and the true nature and destiny of man.

The individualism of the Renaissance began the destruction of this synthesis, despite the heroic attempt of some movements of the Reformation to preserve it upon a new theological and political basis. Shattered in the wars of religion, what remained of the old synthesis disappeared in the first decades of the modern world. Furthermore, the breaking-apart of the medieval "one-world" into the many omnicompetent states of modern Europe was an external symbol of the inner and more serious fragmentation that sundered various aspects of man's thought and activity. Religion, divorced from life, was thrust into one compartment, while science, economics, education, and the arts expressed the growing individualism in their struggles for freedom from each other. The most serious tensions in the culture of our own day have arisen out of the competing claims to absolute autonomy made by these various branches of man's thought and activity. The baffling frustrations which mark our age have come, partly at least, from attempts to find a synthesis while still ignoring the only enduring basis upon which it can be erected: *the Christian religion that affirms God's continuous activity in all areas of His creation.*

The Church in the modern world adjusted itself to the subordinate position where it was thrust by the dominant forces of secularist and humanist idealism. It is easy for us now, painfully educated by the shocking impact of two world wars and the ensuing continuous ideological conflict, to point out precisely where the Church made itself the unconscious handmaid of the very forces that insulated Christianity from the springs of human activity. But what is more important in discerning the pattern of history and in lighting a beacon for the road that lies into the future, is that we should appreciate the astounding vitality of Christianity during this ascendency of secularism. If religion was too often made a purely personal matter, separated from other aspects of man's life and thought, nonetheless Christianity made its influence felt through the lives of those whose personal religion refused to be pigeon-holed. Christian statesmen, Christian scientists, and Christian educators have made the significant contributions to our culture in the past two centuries.

Moreover, never since the days of the first centuries of the Church's life has Christianity displayed such tremendous missionary power as in the modern period. If we are again consciously approaching a "one-world" outlook, it is at least a world that knows in every distant corner the devoted and selfless evangelistic heroism of the modern Christian missionary.

Today the direction of human striving has changed. There is an orientation away from fragmented individualism and once again in the direction of interrelated community. This is the real significance of the various totalitarian movements which have sprung up in the last generation or two. They seek to provide meaning in man's life in terms of some kind of human community. With Christianity banished from the secular idealism which gave birth to these movements, it is not surprising that the basis upon which they attempt to erect a synthesis is some political, racial, or economic interpretation of life. Their strength has been in their appeal to those deepest yearnings of man for membership in a community that at once transcends the individual, and yet offers meaning to his life in relation to the whole. Their fatal weakness, however, lies in that to which they relate man. An abiding common life cannot be built upon purely secularist or humanistic foundations. In one sense these totalitarian movements are horrible parodies of Christianity. Their basic appeal to the instinct of human brotherhood is an appeal to something abiding and eternal in the nature of man, but something that cannot exist in fulfilment except it be related to its source in Almighty God.

The challenging opportunity before the Christian Church in the modern world is to provide human community upon the only sure foundation on which it can be erected in freedom, liberty, and justice—on the religion of the Incarnation. There is today a *fulness of time* in the world quite as striking as that which St. Paul once found in the ancient world. In the seeming chaos into which we are plunged the pattern of history is still clear to the Christian. The Church girds itself for the redemptive task of bringing to birth that human community whose common life rests upon the community of man with God in Christ.

With these preliminary remarks in mind, we shall perhaps be better equipped to survey the chief events and movements of the history of the Modern Church, finding in the imperishable vitality of the Christian faith a guide to the paths leading the Church into the world of tomorrow.

## A CENTURY OF EXHAUSTION

THE century following the intense conflict of the end of the Reformation age was one of spiritual exhaustion. The religious passions of men were spent in the devastating struggles of the wars of religion, and by and large the Church everywhere adjusted itself to the position of secondary importance to which the new interests of the modern world reduced the claims of Christianity.

In the Lutheran states, for example, the wholehearted response of faith, characterizing the Protestant profession of two generations earlier, disappeared. In its place was left an arid and formal orthodoxy of intellectual assent. Likewise, the zealous fervor of the Calvinist no longer stirred men. Internal dissension, generally in the form of theological controversy, occupied and divided members of the Reformed Churches.

Nor was this exhaustion confined to Protestantism. The energies and resources of the Roman Church, once the Counter-Reformation had run its course, were largely devoted to a struggle to recover the power and privileges formerly enjoyed by Catholicism in the European states. Deeply embroiled in the political affairs of the nations, Rome waged a ceaseless, losing battle against those movements, whether democratic or absolutist, that threatened the last vestiges of her ancient control over man's common life. With more to lose than Protestantism, perhaps the papacy was the more sensitive to the insulation of religion from the political, economic, and cultural aspects of man's life.

The Church of England presented no exception to the general picture. The uncompromising Laudian Anglicanism of the early seventeenth century enjoyed a brief revival after the restoration of the monarchy in 1660. By the end of the century, however, it had proved unable to maintain itself against the prevailing currents of secularist thought. With the coming of the Hanoverian kings in the first quarter of the eighteenth century, a paralyzing state control placed the Established Church in a position of lassitude and ineffectiveness.

The intellectual atmosphere of these early years of the modern world was an exciting continuation of the Renaissance emancipation from all medieval sanctions and patterns of thought. Enormous strides were made in the study of the physical sciences in the years between Copernicus and Newton, while a new political philosophy was finding expression in the writings of Hobbes and Locke. Mechanistic philosophers, deists, and advocates of a natural religion alike breathed the rationalism of an Age of Enlightenment in which the dogmatisms of centuries were rejected.

In such an atmosphere the concept of the National Church, born of the Reformation, ceased to have significance for men, though the surviving state-established Churches clung anachronistically to theoretic principles having little counterpart in reality. The unity of a citizenry in religion was no longer deemed essential to the national welfare, nor to their unity in a common political loyalty. It was this breakdown of the National Church idea which accelerated the divisions of Protestantism, already begun in the period of the wars of religion. With religion more and more reduced to a purely private and individual concern, and the principle of independency or congregational autonomy exercising an increasingly important influence, the sects and denominations of Protestant Christianity grew constantly more numerous.

Yet late in the early seventeenth century it was Protestantism that responded first to the challenge of the new secular order. A spiritual awakening began in Germany, destined to have far-reaching consequences in the whole Protestant world.

## THE PIETIST AWAKENING

THE rekindling of Christian devotion and activity that spread through German Lutheranism as Protestantism found a new spiritual strength gave rise to a movement called Pietism. Philip Jacob Spener, August Hermann Francke, and the other leaders, nearly all men connected with German seminary and university life, made their influence felt in Dresden, Berlin, Leipzig, and Halle.

Pietism was essentially a resurgence of the unquenchable evangelical spirit in Christianity. As in the Middle Ages from time to time evangelical groups broke out in protest against the institutionalism of the papal Church, so now in Protestant Germany the evangelical witness of Christianity stirred itself in protest against the formalistic intellectual religion of later Lutheranism. Once again the individual response of faith and self-dedication was proclaimed as the central feature of the Christian profession. A response of wholehearted self-commitment to Christ, it was expressed in the conscious psychological experience of conversion. The prayer groups of Pietists recovered not only the Scriptures as the supreme guide and initial force in personal religion, but also the spiritual treasures in the writings of pre-Reformation German mystics. These, with their emphasis upon an intuitive and direct knowledge of God without the sacramental and formal observances of the institutional Church, had perhaps a greater effect upon the new Protestant spirituality than they ever had upon the ordinary religious life of the Medieval Church.

The most interesting figure in this movement is that of a German nobleman, Count Nicholas von Zinzendorf, the godson of Philip Spener and a man whose whole life was devoted to the ardent evangelicalism of the Pietists. Toward the middle of the eighteenth century Zinzendorf gave shelter on his vast Saxon estates to the surviving members of a Church then three centuries old, the brotherhood known as *Unitas fratrum*. These were the Moravian Brethren who had separated themselves from Rome shortly after the days of John Hus in Bohemia. Driven from place to place in central Europe, reduced to a faithful remnant by the bitter conflict of the wars of religion, they at last found a haven of safety.

Zinzendorf became aware of the reservoir of spiritual strength in this ancient body of Christians, tenacious of their conservative Church life and raised to a high level of spirituality under the impact of continuous persecution. To them he brought the warm, emotional, personal religion of Pietism. The fusion of these influences produced in the Church of the Moravian Brethren the finest flowering of early Protestant evangelicalism. Their closely knit organization gave power and direction to their enterprises; their freedom from any national or local background allowed them to disperse their influence throughout many areas of non-Roman Christendom. It was not surprising to find Moravians among the leaders in the missionary activity that sprang from the evangelical awakening, but the scope of their efforts to spread the Gospel in the modern world is truly remarkable. The century following the reconstitution of the Moravian Brethren by Zinzendorf in 1747 saw the heroic Moravian mission spread from South Africa to Greenland, from Pennsylvania to the East Indies.

There is a link between the Pietist awakening in Germany and the *Evangelical Movement* which stirred the Church of England in the eighteenth century. One-half of that link was forged by the outreaching influence of the Moravians. The other half was provided by the personal activity of a man who came under the compelling attraction of their evangelicalism, John Wesley. More than anyone else he was responsible for the spiritual awakening that swept away the religious lethargy of Englishmen.

### ENGLAND IN THE EIGHTEENTH CENTURY

BY THE end of the first quarter of the eighteenth century the Church of England had ceased to be an effective spiritual or moral force in the national life. Giving the appearance of simply one more traditional English institution, the Hanoverian Church has become proverbial for its religious somnolence. Much as this decline may be exaggerated, it is undeniably true that there was serious administrative corruption and religious decay within the life of the Establishment.

Neglect of pastoral care and parochial duty was widespread. Preaching had declined; the sacraments were infrequently celebrated. The picture one encounters of the eighteenth-century parson, a "three-bottle man" at the squire's table, striding into the village church with his surplice scarce concealing his riding habit, laying aside his crop momentarily to hasten through the service with an officious and beery parish clerk, is hardly typical. But on the other hand, the clerical figures whom Jane Austen presents or who people the pages of Trollope's Barchester novels, though perhaps more refined, are scarcely more attractive as the servants of Jesus Christ.

In many ways the tone of the Hanoverian Church was reflected in the character of its episcopate. The average eighteenth century bishop was an inoffensive, learned, but dull man, selected for office because of his connection with some aristocratic or respectable old county family and his reliability as a Whig voter in the House of Lords. Attendance at the latter was his chief occupation, requiring a long residence in London. A few months only were left him for episcopal governance and care of his diocese.

The wonder is not that there were so few eighteenth-century bishops who achieved any degree of intellectual or ecclesiastical eminence, but rather that a surprising number did so, despite the handicaps of the circumstances. William Wake, the canonist and patristic historian; Joseph Butler, whose *Analogy of Religion* was a decisive refutation of the position of the deists and became one of the classic works of Anglican theology; George Berkeley, the Irish bishop and philosopher; Thomas Sherlock, perhaps the best of the eighteenth-century churchmen, whose farsighted attempts to secure an episcopate for the American Colonies were thwarted by the Whig politicians— these would be distinguished men in any age. But it is not from them that the eighteenth-century Church received its tone.

Three forces combined to place the English Church in this unhappy condition, the first of which needs no further discussion. It was the impact of those secularist elements in men's thought, already described as characteristic of the century following the Reformation. It is worth noting that the paralyzing effect of the Age of Enlightenment was felt in both the surviving remnant of English Romanists and the larger body of Dissenters, as well as in the Established Church.

Peculiar to the National Church, however, was the paradox presented by a reformed Church whose institutional life was still that of three centuries earlier. The Reformation had left virtually untouched much of the old ecclesiastical administrative machinery. Throughout the eighteenth century and into the first quarter of the nineteenth, while England took on the aspect and activity of a modern industrial state, the Church in her external institutions was still the Church of the Tudor period. There were many areas where the Reformation had done little to right the evils, inequities, and abuses of all sorts. The evils of plurality, the practice of a clergyman holding more than one benefice and absenteeism still hampered the Church in the pastoral care of the people. An inflexible system of diocesan and parochial boundaries, the inheritance of by-gone centuries, prevented any adequate ministry to a population increased in numbers, and now rapidly shifting to the new commercial and manufacturing cities. Privilege was deeply intrenched in church life. The cathedrals, for example, supported dozens of canons whose posts were handsomely endowed sinecures, while hundreds of rural clergy, despite the funds provided by the generosity of Queen Anne, maintained a starveling existence.

The political and social reform movement of the early nineteenth century extended itself to the ecclesiastical institution, bringing many of these abuses to an end, but until that had been done the condition of the eighteenth-century Church was in some measure due to the incompleteness of the Reformation.

The final force that deprived the Church of much of its spiritual power in the days of the Hanoverian monarchs was the blatant Erastianism[1] of the age. The Tudor princes with their doctrine of royal supremacy exercised a decisive control of the religious life of the nation through the Establishment. The Georges, or rather, their ministers of state, exercised a decisive control over the Establishment which very nearly divorced it entirely from the religious life of the nation. Few events, for example, had such a crippling effect upon the activity of the Church as the silencing of Convocation by George I in 1717. For more than a century and a quarter the Church of England did not meet in synod to consider and act upon the problems, opportunities, and challenges that the times placed before the Church. It is almost impossible to imagine the effects of this arbitrary use of the state's power. If a modern Episcopalian were to try to imagine the condition of his Church after a hundred years in which there were no meetings of General or Diocesan Conventions, little activity at National Headquarters, few organizations beyond those of the immediate parish, he might come to understand with more sympathy the condition to which the Church of England found herself reduced two hundred years ago.

### JOHN WESLEY AND THE METHODISTS

In 1729 a small group of serious-minded young men at Oxford formed a religious association which the more mundane of their contemporaries speedily nicknamed "The Holy Club." There was little that was remarkable in

---

[1] *Erastianism* is the term popularly used to describe the doctrine of state supremacy in ecclesiastical affairs. It may be noted that the views of Erastus, a sixteenth-century Swiss theologian, are not accurately reproduced in the idea of complete state control which men called by his name.

this fellowship, save perhaps that it ran counter to the spirit of the age. Certainly there was no hint that one day one of the largest communions of Protestant Christendom would trace its origin to the members of this group. Primarily an ascetic association, the band of young men sought to deepen their own spiritual lives by the Church's prescribed exercises of prayer and fasting, by Bible reading, a weekly communion, and other devotions that were then branded as "high church."

The moving spirits in the group were the Wesley brothers, Charles and John, sons of the rector of Epworth. The rule or spiritual method (hence *Methodist*) by which the members of the fellowship lived was devised by these two ardent and devoted churchmen. Thus the Holy Club was not initially an evangelistic organization, but much more a devotional confraternity. Its historical importance derives from its effect upon John Wesley. Long after this obscure fellowship had broken up, there remained with him the disciplined devotion nurtured in this experience, and which later, after his conversion, empowered and directed his new-found evangelistic zeal.

Wesley had been ordained as a Fellow of Lincoln College, Oxford, but in 1735, his restless spiritual quest unsatisfied by English parochial and university life, he accepted an invitation to go out as a missionary to James Oglethorpe's new American colony of Georgia. Here he was miserable and disillusioned. Neither the rough and worldly settlers nor the Indians, already debauched by the white man, cared for the austere religion and strict ecclesiastical discipline of a former member of the Holy Club. But it was in Georgia that Wesley met the Moravians.

Impressed by their quiet piety and unswerving zeal for the Gospel, he sought out the Moravian colony in London upon his return to England. Under their influence, in 1738 John Wesley suffered the experience of conversion, finding both inward peace and a new outward evangelistic vocation in his assurance of the companionship of Christ.

The story of the spread of the Evangelical Movement and its reinvigorating effects throughout England is well-known. Wesley, George Whitefield, and the other impassioned leaders plunged into the neglected areas of England's growing commercial and industrial activity, preaching Christ to crowds that were numbered literally in the thousands. In a few years nearly the entire country was swept with hysterical religious enthusiasm.

The spirit of the age, however, offered a certain natural resistance to the new religious movement, perhaps expressed best in the remark of Samuel Johnson that you could not tell where you were with a man who claimed "to have the Inner Light." Active organized opposition was present as well. The day had not passed when men feared the political power of a religious movement. Though events proved these fears groundless, there was widespread suspicion that this uncontrollable revival might become a revolutionary political force. Furthermore, the opposition of the Established Church was intense. Its pulpits were closed to the revivalist preachers; its beneficed clergy denounced the enthusiasm with violent invective. For its failure to understand and relate to itself this Methodist movement, the Church of England has been much criticized. Yet it is doubtful whether the eighteenth-century Church possessed either the flexibility or the freedom to incorporate the new religious forces wholly within its own life.

After all, despite the fact that John Wesley remained to the end of his life a clergyman of the Church of England, Methodism presented a twofold challenge to the principles of Anglicanism. First, the essential Wesleyan doctrine of the necessity of a conversion experience contained implications seriously at variance with the sacramental or Catholic character of the Anglican institution. There were doctrinal emphases within Methodism that were more closely akin to the principles of Dissent than to those of the Establishment. Secondly, the religious societies which were formed of those who had been converted showed independent and separatist tendencies from the very beginning. By no means all their members were drawn from Anglican ranks. Many came from dissenting bodies or were folk whose religious loyalty could only be vaguely defined as Protestant. It is not surprising, then, that the early evangelicals made a false distinction; they were Christians before they were Churchmen.

By the year 1760 the separatist tendencies were actively at work. Appealing to the rights afforded by the English Act of Toleration to those who could not conform to the Church of England, the Wesleyans began to license their meeting-halls as Dissenting Chapels. Steadily for three decades the movement toward independent organization grew. One stream of the Evangelical Movement remained within the life of the Church of England; the other broke away from the fringes of both Anglicanism and Dissent to form what is known today as the Methodist Church. In 1784 John Wesley, then eighty-one years old, began to ordain a ministry for the new body, an act marking the complete independency of Methodism. Wesley himself remained its only link with the Establishment until his death in 1791.

## THE CHURCH EVANGELICALS

WITHIN the life of the Church of England, however, a more sober stream of the Evangelical Movement was exercising a reinvigorating influence. Wesley is the romantic and commanding figure of this whole revival, but many of the loyal and devoted Church evangelicals deserve better than the obscurity into which they have passed. William Romaine touched the lives of hundreds by his compelling preaching in the city churches of London, while Henry Venn demonstrated in Yorkshire that the evangelical witness could be a vigorous part of the Anglican heritage.

Their successors carried the influence of this awakening within the Establishment to even greater lengths. The gentle and holy Charles Simeon of Cambridge had a profound influence on that important university center. Hannah More, with her schools and religious literature, was the very embodiment of the evangelical concern with Christian education. Most influential of all was the Clapham group of London professional men, headed by William Wilberforce. Under the influence of their rector, John Venn, they expressed their Christian conviction in untiring philanthropic activity and the zealous championship of causes of social reform. The Evangelical Movement can make a just claim to such widely divergent fruits of its activity as the modern Sunday School system and the abolition of the slave trade in British possessions.

Indeed, there were few areas of England's life that had not felt the influence of the revival by the end of the eighteenth century. At long last the Church was making a spiritual impact upon the nation. The moral earnestness of the evangelicals raised the standards of society; their passion for justice was reflected in the wide opinion gathering behind the movement for social and economic reform. In their philanthropic activity they reached out to touch the poor and the underprivileged both in the cottages of the countryside and in the crowded slums of the cities. Concern for the Christian mission, so inseparably a part of this evangelical witness, found its outlet in the formation in 1799 of the Church Missionary Society, the famous C.M.S., which was destined to play a vital role in the overseas expansion of Anglicanism.

The historian cannot ignore the fact that the effectiveness of the Evangelical Movement was assisted by the changing external circumstances of the last decades of the eighteenth century. A disturbing insecurity, aggravated by the writings of men like Thomas Paine, had seized men's minds. The collapse of the old régime in France underlined the extent to which revolutionary political thought had spread throughout Europe, and the protracted struggle against Napoleon, in which England often seemed to stand alone, accentuated the insecurity of the times. Men saw in the Church both a refuge from the world's disturbances and a bulwark against the spread of new and subversive ideas. To recognize these conditions is not to detract from the very real accomplishments of the whole Protestant awakening, but rather to see it in the historical setting that intensified its force.

## THE EXPANSION OF CHRISTIANITY

ONE of the significant results of the evangelical awakening throughout the Protestant world was the tremendous missionary enterprise of the nineteenth century. Catholic zeal for missions, aroused by the Counter-Reformation, had carried the Roman Church westwards to the New World and eastwards to the Indies in the earlier days of exploration and conquest. Now it was the turn of Protestantism. Though the nineteenth century witnessed a renewal of missionary activity in the Roman Church, the real glory of this period in which the Gospel was carried to every quarter of the globe belongs to non-Roman Christianity.

Nothing was more characteristic of the Victorian Age than the bands of heroic and self-sacrificing men and women who were to be found in every far corner of the world, laboring in Christ's name to enlighten the minds, heal the bodies, and save the souls of "the heathen in his blindness." A sophisticated generation smiles with faint amusement at the naïveté of the familiar missionary hymn *From Greenland's Icy Mountains,* but the very simplicity of its lines sprang from a single-minded evangelistic devotion on a scale that Christianity had seldom before known. Cheerfully accepting what was then virtually permanent exile, hundreds of Christians endured incredible hardship and suffering, often involving martyrdom itself, to work on the tropical shores of the South Seas or in some remote hinterland of continental Asia and Africa. There they built schools and hospitals, translated the Scriptures, frequently making a written language out of a spoken dialect to do so, and made known the redemptive love of God in Jesus Christ.

Exploration and conquest opened up the vast stretches of inner Africa, and missionaries from all Christian bodies followed their national flags in the wake of imperialist expansion and annexation. China's ports saw the entry of foreigners in 1842, though missionaries were at work there before that date. If the first Chinese contacts with Western nations were darkened by the horrors of the opium trade and ruthless exploitation, they were at least partly redeemed by the unselfish activity of the missionaries. Christian workers entered Japan in 1859, first as doctors and educators, for it was not until the publication of the Imperial Edict of Toleration in 1873 that direct evangelistic activity was permitted. Meanwhile, missionaries had been at work since the turn of the century among the tribal people of New Zealand and the far-flung Melanesian and Polynesian Islands of the South Pacific.

The remarkable expansion of Christianity saw some significant changes in the character of the missionary enterprise. The effort of evangelism was broadened, chiefly through education and medical services, to make an impact upon the whole man and the society in which he lived. While very often *westernization* was a more obvious result than Christianization, the missionary does not bear the chief blame for the transplanting of the evils of one culture to another. The political and economic forces of imperialism and exploitation, frequently protecting and subsidizing the mission for their own gain, proved impossible to control.

The broadening of the missionary enterprise had the effect, in the long run, of spreading Christian standards and ideals throughout the cultures of people who might not themselves be converted in any great numbers to the Church. Particularly was this true in the East, in India, China, and Japan. The comparatively small number of Christians today in relation to the total population in any of these countries, exercises a decisive and altogether disproportionate influence in the life of the nation. That minority influence rests upon the wide diffusion of Christian principles through the missionary concern with education, medicine, and social reform and amelioration.

Equally important were the changes in attitude toward missionary responsibility which took place in all the Churches, Catholic and Protestant alike. For the first time since the days before Constantine's recognition of Christianity, the spread of the Gospel became part of the vocation of the rank and file of lay folk. Missions were supported financially upon an increasingly broader base of Christian giving. Thousands of Church people found in the new missionary societies and agencies the means whereby they could participate, at least indirectly, in what was felt to be the final and irresistible expansion of the faith.

The shattering impact of the first World War disorganized the whole missionary enterprise and challenged the optimistic idealism upon which much of the evangelizing effort had been allowed to rest. The disillusioning era of conflict and insecurity that followed, culminating in the outbreak of another World War, destroyed the lingering shreds of any purely humanistic idealism and revealed the frightening extent to which the modern world had become secularized. Yet for the Christian Mission the tragic world situation today presents a challenging opportunity such as Christendom has not known for a thousand years. On all sides the hunger for human community is manifest. Yet the thoughtful Christian today knows that ideals are not enough. Only in that divinely ordered community, empowered by the presence of Jesus Christ—His Church—can man find a membership that gives meaning to his life and which has a redemptive effect upon the other memberships, racial and cultural, social and political, comprising the complex pattern of civilization. The world lies open today to the proclamation of the final human community in Christ. It is that Gospel which has lighted man through the darkest hours of history.

## THE CHURCH OF ENGLAND OVERSEAS

WHILE the overseas expansion of Anglicanism anticipated the great missionary movement of Protestant Christendom by a century or more, it cannot be said that this initial expansion of the Church of England was truly missionary. Rather, the English Church went overseas with Englishmen. The work of the Society for the Promotion of Christian Knowledge, founded in 1699 "to promote religion and learning in any part of His Majesty's Plantations abroad," was motivated chiefly by a desire to serve English colonists. At the outset, at least, this was also true of the Society for the Propagation of the Gospel, formed in 1701. The S.P.G., for example, was responsible for a large measure of the support of Anglican clergy who served the churches in the American Colonies or became official chaplains in the settlements of the East India Company, but in both instances the primary concern was with English nationals under the British flag.

On the other hand, missionary work with the savage

and non-Christian peoples who were encountered by the settlers was at least contemplated by the S.P.G. The Society encouraged its clergy to undertake the conversion of the natives wherever possible, and the Bishops of London, under whose remote jurisdiction the overseas Church was placed, made an occasional inquiry concerning progress in such work. Little, however, was actually accomplished. The policy of the directors of the East India Company during the eighteenth century was opposed to evangelization, while in the American Colonies the relations between the settlers and the Indians placed almost insurmountable obstacles in the way of the conversion of the latter. A notable exception was the famous Mohawk Mission in western New York, inaugurated to prevent these Indians from "being practiced upon by French priests and Jesuits." The Board of Trade and Plantations cared little about the ecclesiastical loyalties of any Indians who might become Christians; what mattered was their loyalty to the British in the French and Indian Wars.

By the time of the formation of the Church Missionary Society in 1799, under the impetus of the Evangelical Movement, the situation had changed. S.P.G. and C.M.S. alike devoted their increasing resources to missionary work. In the early years of the nineteenth century when Anglicanism was carried overseas by colonial settlers, it went with a keen sense of evangelistic responsibility to the non-Christian peoples of the British Empire. More important, Anglicanism almost immediately emancipated itself from the British flag, demonstrating its essential catholicity in a vigorous expansion beyond the spheres of English influence and limits of Anglo-Saxon peoples.

The Anglican Communion as we know it today has come into being out of a century and a half of such overseas expansion of the Church of England. In many ways the eighteen independent Churches and Provinces that are united in a common faith and order to form this worldwide fellowship differ considerably from each other. The Anglican Church of Canada, for example, as well as the Church of England in Australia and Tasmania, and the Church in the Province of New Zealand, were all formed by the transplantation of the Church of England to overseas colonies by English settlers. On the other hand, while the Church of the Province of the West Indies and the Church of India, Burma, Pakistan, and Ceylon originated in this manner, so remarkable has been the progress of evangelization of non-Christians that these Churches have a truly indigenous appearance. Two of the autonomous bodies of the Communion *Chung Hua Sheng Kung Hui* (The Chinese Church) and *Nippon Sei Ko Kwai* (The Holy Catholic Church of Japan) came into being through the joint missionary efforts of the English, American, and Canadian Churches. Today they are Chinese and Japanese in character.

One of the most notable areas of Anglican missionary work in the past century has been the African continent. Except for the mission of the Episcopal Church in Liberia, this extensive venture has been nearly entirely the work of the Church of England. Today no less than five separate Anglican Provinces, each with its own group of dioceses, as well as some adjacent missionary districts, stretch from Cairo down to Capetown on the east side of the continent, and include large areas of former British colonies on the west African coast. The overwhelming number of clergy in these dioceses and missionary areas are natives, more than five hundred in all. In our time, with the coming of political freedom and the realization of national aspirations by so many Africans, the fact that African Anglicanism is increasingly a church of African peoples has helped to separate Christianity from the former colonialism of western nations.

The first independent Church in the Anglican Communion outside the British Isles was that formed out of the American colonial parishes and missions after the Revolution: The Protestant Episcopal Church. Indeed, with the appearance of this autonomous sister-church in another land, the Anglican Communion itself came into being.

## THE ENGLISH CHURCH IN COLONIAL AMERICA

THE attitude toward religion differed markedly in the various American colonies during the century and a half before their independence of Great Britain. America was settled during the wars of religion and their immediate aftermath. It was altogether natural, therefore, that various groups of colonists should bring with them the conflicting religious loyalties of Europe in the seventeenth century. These formed the background and decisively affected the planting of the Church of England in the American colonial scene.

In the Massachusetts Bay Colony of New England, for example, where the Puritans had established the Calvinist theocracy denied them at home by the early Stuart monarchs, the services of the detested Prayer Book were outlawed. Clergy who used the liturgy or defended the principles of Anglicanism were expelled from the settlements. Civil disabilities were imposed upon those who did not meet the rigid Puritan qualifications for "good religious folk." Even after the accession of William III had secured some measure of religious freedom for those loyal to the Church of England, Puritan preachers still branded King's Chapel in Boston, with Old Testament vehemence, as a "High Place" with its "Priest of Baal."

It was not until the early years of the eighteenth century that Anglicans came to occupy any significant place in the life of the Massachusetts colony. Then, with the liberal assistance of the S.P.G., Church parishes began to be formed with increasing rapidity. But Puritan Congregationalism, with its singular adaptability to the conditions of pioneer life, was by that time deeply intrenched among the people of New England. Anglican parishes existed in all the chief centers of New England before the American Revolution, and with considerable strength in Connecticut. Yet they were often regarded as the churches of the folk of wealth and quality, those suspected of loyalty to the crown during the struggle for independence.

On the other hand, the colonial settlements of Virginia presented an entirely different religious picture. From the first establishment of the colony in the early seventeenth century, Anglicanism was placed in a privileged position, both by the regulations of the Virginia Company and the later ecclesiastical laws of the colonial Assembly. Pre-revolutionary Virginian life, in many aspects a conscious transplantation of that of England, had its Established Church. Local civil administration was parochial; grants of glebe land and tithes on the staple crop, tobacco, supported the clergy.

Obviously, considerable modification and adaptation of the Establishment took place in America, especially in the administrative and disciplinary areas of the Church's life. No ecclesiastical courts existed to give effective implementation to the canon law. More important, in the absence of immediate episcopal oversight, both the authority of the civil government in ecclesiastical affairs and the powers of lay vestries were greatly increased. However much this gave rise to a number of abuses in colonial Church life, eventually it produced considerable local initiative and a sense of lay responsibility, elements that played a decisive part in the organization of the scattered Anglican parishes after the American Revolution.

Other forms of religious settlement in the colonies ranged between these extremes of Anglican Virginia and Puritan Massachusetts. In South Carolina a Church of England establishment existed on the Virginia model. Maryland, after a policy of religious toleration had been maintained for some years, saw Anglicanism established at the end of the seventeenth century when the proprietary settlement became a royal colony. Georgia passed an act establishing the Anglican Church in 1758, but it was scarcely more than the legal machinery for effective civil administration in the townships or parishes. Anglicanism was so weak in comparison with dissenting Protestant bodies as to be of little religious importance in Georgia.

Northwards, conditions in most of New England resembled those in Massachusetts, except for the unusual Anglican strength in Connecticut and the principles of complete religious liberty and total separation of Church and State that guided the founders of Rhode Island. In the Middle Atlantic colonies, from New York to Pennsylvania, Anglican parishes were securely founded without the assistance of civil establishments. Actually, a theoretical establishment was introduced in some parts of New York by an Assembly Act of 1693, but its operation was limited and the strength of the Church did not rest upon its preferred legal position.

It is a mistake to imagine that the Anglican parishes in America reproduced all the features of Church life in the mother country. Even in Virginia, where the effort at transplantation was greatest, the frontier conditions of colonial life inevitably affected the Church. The self-reliant, democratic spirit of pioneer America became quite as characteristic of the colonial Anglican as it was of his Puritan or Congregationalist neighbor. Responsible lay participation in the affairs of the parishes, and in some cases, control of them, was common. This modification of the English ecclesiastical system was intensified by the subtle influences of the strong Puritan and Independent groups upon the Anglican minority. Wherever the Church of England put down its deepest roots among the people of the colonies, it shared in those differences that were beginning to distinguish the American from his English cousin.

The most serious barrier in the way of the growth and expansion of Anglicanism in America was the lack of an episcopate. For more than a century and a half there was no bishop in the colonial Church to provide leadership, episcopal ministration, and coördination of ecclesiastical life. The anomaly of the parishes of an Episcopal Church living under the theoretical jurisdiction of a bishop three thousand miles away is hard to imagine or to understand. The difficulties it raised were frustrating in the extreme. Men who sought ordination to the ministry were forced to undertake the long and arduous journey across the Atlantic and back. No effective supervision could be exercised over the parishes.

Repeated attempts were made, both by the S.P.G. and by farsighted Bishops of London, to end this intolerable situation. But to all these the English government turned a deaf ear. The Whig ministers of the eighteenth century were well aware of the colonial Puritans' fear that bishops might be clothed with more than "spiritual powers only." Moreover, the opposition of American dissenters was strengthened by the hostility of their English brethren. At the same time, the state of the Established Church in the eighteenth century, already described, made impossible any concerted effort on the part of churchmen to overcome this essentially political opposition. The formation of an American episcopate was thus postponed until after American political independence.

## THE PROTESTANT EPISCOPAL CHURCH [1a]

THE Revolution that separated the colonies of the Atlantic seaboard from the English crown left the Anglican congregations isolated from the mother Church. The scattered parishes were completely disorganized and suffered

---

[1a] Detailed treatment of the history, structure, and activity of the Episcopal Church is provided in Volume VI in this series, entitled *The Episcopal Church and Its Work* (Revised Edition, 1961).

acute financial distress. The civil establishments guaranteeing the support of the Church in the southern colonies were terminated by the new States; in the north the funds provided by the S.P.G. were necessarily withdrawn. Moreover, the flight of a large number of Loyalists from the central and New England States to Canada and the West Indies removed from the Church many of its ablest clergy and lay leaders.

At this moment, however, Anglicanism gave proof of its vitality as the local initiative and sense of responsibility that had developed under the peculiar American conditions demonstrated itself. The American congregations launched themselves upon a bold experiment—the formation of a free and independent Church of the Anglican Communion, the first of its kind outside the British Isles, and one destined to serve as a model for the other autonomous Anglican bodies that have come into being during the past century.

Between 1780 and 1783, the Rev. William White of Philadelphia ₁and the Rev. William Smith of Maryland took steps to organize the clergy and laymen of the Middle States into The Protestant Episcopal Church, appealing to parishes elsewhere to join them. Meanwhile, the clergy of Connecticut, firmly convinced that no national organization should be completed until an American episcopate had been secured, sent the Rev. Samuel Seabury to England to seek consecration as bishop.

Though Seabury was courteously received, the existing ecclesiastical laws prevented the English bishops from consecrating a man who could not take the statutory oaths of allegiance and supremacy. As a result, Seabury went to

Scotland. There, on November 14, 1784, he was consecrated by three bishops of the little independent Scottish Episcopal Church, a body which had continued an heroic and precarious existence in Presbyterian Scotland ever since the revolution of 1688 had swept episcopacy out of the Church of Scotland.

The legal obstacles which prevented Seabury's consecration in England aroused the English archbishops to action. Within two years Parliament was persuaded to pass the enabling legislation that allowed William White and Samuel Provoost to be consecrated in Lambeth Palace Chapel in 1787 for the Dioceses of Pennsylvania and New York. In 1790 the American episcopate in the English line was completed by the consecration of James Madison.

The General Convention of 1789 saw the final achievement of national unity and organization in the Protestant Episcopal Church. Earlier conventions in 1785 and 1786, attacking the problems facing the Church, had laid the groundwork for their solution. In 1789 the adoption of the Prayer Book and the Constitution gave the American Church the formularies in which its doctrine, discipline, and worship were enshrined. Anglicanism was no longer confined to Great Britain. It had demonstrated a truly Catholic capacity to adapt itself to new conditions and circumstances, and yet maintain the continuity of its own tradition with the historic life of the Church.

## THE CHARACTER OF THE EPISCOPAL CHURCH

CONSTITUTIONALLY, the Episcopal Church restored the ancient principle of Church government through representative synods, with the significant admission of laymen to a direct voice and vote in the affairs of the Church. The governing bodies were the conventions, formed of bishops and elected representatives of the clerical and lay orders.

The Constitution of 1789 provided for a triennial General Convention, composed of a House of Bishops and a House of Clerical and Lay Deputies. This was the supreme national synod. Locally, each diocese (an area at first coterminous with each State) would meet annually in its own Diocesan Convention, presided over by the bishop, and composed of clergy and elected lay representatives of the parishes and missions within the area. A large measure of autonomy and independence was accorded the several dioceses. Perhaps it is more accurate to say that the dioceses agreed to sacrifice some of their jealously guarded independence in order to create a national organization. Actually, the Episcopal Church was a federal union of independent diocesan units, and each diocese a federation of independent parishes, rather than a single, closely knit ecclesiastical institution. This kind of organization was natural in a Church whose new constitutional life was shaped at the same time and under the same influences that created a federal government for the sovereign States of the new American Republic.

During the past century and a half, as the dioceses of the Episcopal Church have expanded from a narrow strip of territory along the Atlantic seaboard to cover the whole area of the United States, some serious defects in the original organization have been displayed. To retain the parallel with American political life, while the States through the years have surrendered a large part of their original sovereignty to the national government, the dioceses have remained in a federal system. Thus while the constitutional provisions for democratic and representative Church government placed a curb upon the ancient prelatical powers of the bishop as sole ruler of his diocese, they did not succeed in relating the diocese effectively to the administrative and evangelistic life of the whole Church. Diocesan independence, like parochialism, has too often displayed itself only in self-concern. It is no exaggeration to say that this has been one of the chief obstacles to the effective missionary work of the National Church, both at home and abroad.

In so far as it was applicable to local situations, the Anglican Church in the colonies was subject to the English canon law as embodied in the post-Reformation revision known as *The Canons of 1604.* Naturally the greater part of this code ceased to be relevant to the independent American Church. Revision was undertaken almost at once, and has continued through the years. Today, like nearly all the autonomous Churches of the Anglican Communion, the Episcopal Church possesses its own *Constitution and Canons,* governing and regulating various aspects of its life. These canons not only embody the enactments of General Convention specifically directed toward situations peculiar to the American scene, but also preserve in the tradition of the Episcopal Church much of that ancient heritage of discipline and custom that has marked the life of the Christian Church for centuries.

"This Church is far from intending to depart from the Church of England in any essential point of doctrine, discipline, or worship"—such was the principle that guided the leaders of the American Church in 1789 and was placed by them in the Preface to the first American Prayer Book. Perhaps nowhere is that principle so clearly seen at work as in the Prayer Book itself.

## THE AMERICAN PRAYER BOOK

THE changes made in the English *Book of Common Prayer* to enable its use by the newly organized American Church were few. Prayers for the King, no longer appropriate, were turned into supplications for the President and for the civil magistrates of the States. Slight alterations in phraseology removed obsolete words throughout the liturgical offices, and a few new occasional prayers were authorized.

The one significant change in the old Prayer Book was the incorporation of the Consecration Prayer from the service of Holy Communion set forth by the Scottish Episcopal Church in 1764. Bishop Seabury, faithful to an agreement made with his Scottish consecrators, had used this prayer in an *Order for the Holy Communion* issued in 1786 for use in his diocese. Thence it found its way into the Prayer Book of 1789, and was the first of many changes that have restored in the course of time much of the form and spirit of Cranmer's first English Prayer Book of 1549 to the authorized liturgy of the Protestant Episcopal Church.

Subsequent revisions of the American Book of Common Prayer were completed in 1892 and 1928. In each case, after prolonged study and discussion, during which the renewed interest of Churchmen in the history and meaning of Christian worship became apparent, alterations were made in the direction of greater flexibility of use and spiritual enrichment of the services.[2] Today it is at last realized that continuous liturgical revision is both inevitable and desirable. There can be nothing static in the forms of worship of a community that seeks its fulfillment as the living Body of Christ. Change comes slowly but surely as each generation of men is led to see wider implications of Christian worship in the social and cultural order in which they live.

## THE EXPANSION OF THE EPISCOPAL CHURCH

Two decades of depressing inaction followed on the heels of the tremendous effort of organizing the Episcopal Church in the new American States. This was due at least in part to the crippling losses in personnel, resources, and prestige which the Church had suffered during the American Revolution. These years, also, were perhaps the inevitable period of adjustment intervening between an older leadership, whose ideas and patterns of thought had been formed in colonial days, and the rise of a new generation of clergy ready to explore the peculiar task of Anglicanism in the American scene.

The year 1811 marks the reawakening and renewed activity of the Episcopal Church. In that year John Henry Hobart and Alexander Viets Griswold were consecrated bishops, of New York and the Eastern Diocese respectively.[3] Not only were both men imaginative, devoted, and indefatigable leaders, but they represented as well those

---

[2] Detailed liturgical discussion is beyond the scope of this book. Reference should be made to the volume in this series entitled *The Worship of the Church*.

[3] The Eastern Diocese at this time was made up of Massachusetts (including Maine), Rhode Island, Vermont, and New Hampshire.

diverse religious forces within the Episcopal Church that combined to make the nineteenth century one of expansion, both at home and abroad.

Griswold was an Evangelical, a man whose quiet simplicity of life and modest bearing concealed a passionate love of Christ and ardor for the conversion of His children. His episcopal activity in the New England States was marked by the zealous missionary outreach characteristic of Anglican evangelicalism. The effect of his long years of labor for the Gospel was to establish the Church on firm foundations in an area that had been the very stronghold of Puritanism. Upon his death in 1843, the vast Eastern Diocese, once but thinly populated with Episcopalians, was sub-divided into independent dioceses in the States of which it had been composed.

John Henry Hobart was a High Churchman of the finest type. Concerned to emphasize the unique character of the Episcopal Church among the non-Roman religious bodies in America, and jealous for the preservation of its historic Catholic heritage, yet he was equally energetic in his proclamation of the Church's evangelistic task. "Evangelical Truth and Apostolic Order!" was Hobart's ringing watchword. The influence of his magnetic personality and farsighted plans for deepening and strengthening the work of the Episcopal Church extended far beyond the Diocese of New York.

Griswold and Hobart inspired a host of men to follow the lead they had given. Bishops Moore and Meade rekindled the fires of devotion in Virginia, Dehon began his vigorous work in South Carolina, while Ravenscroft led the way in North Carolina. Doane in New Jersey, Hopkins in Vermont, Whittingham in Maryland—every diocese along the Eastern seaboard found its leader and showed signs of the general reawakening.

But already the task of the Church had spread beyond the confines of the original colonial settlements. In the second and third decades of the nineteenth century, the forest trails and mountain passes leading to the valleys of the Ohio and the Mississippi were jammed with a flood of settlers. Thousands of families poured into the wide territories of the Middle West. In another generation they would move still further, following the Oregon Trail, toiling over the Rocky Mountains, conquering the last barriers in the overland route to the Pacific.

These pioneer settlements presented the American Churches with a stupendous missionary challenge, an opportunity that many of them were quick to seize. The Presbyterians and Congregationalists made valiant efforts to minister to the migrating hordes, though their influence was perhaps chiefly felt in the educational and cultural areas of frontier life. The Baptist and Methodist Churches were those of greatest religious influence, a fact partly accounting for the large size of these two bodies in American Protestantism today. Less traditional and conservative ecclesiastically, more flexible in their organization—especially in their capacity to utilize the services of circuit-riding evangelists and lay preachers—more easily adaptable to the general conditions of frontier life, the Baptists and the Methodists won thousands of adherents among the settlers. Side by side with these bodies there sprang up the numerous revivalist and millennial sects that are the peculiar phenomena of American Christianity. Often short-lived, and sometimes bizarre in the extreme, nevertheless the tempestuous spiritual and emotional forces that these sects unleashed left a permanent mark upon religious life in America.

The Episcopal Church was but slowly aroused to the challenge of the new West, though here and there individuals were to be found who were alive to the importance of the work beyond the mountains. Philander Chase, for example, made his first missionary journey to the West in 1802, and became Bishop of Ohio in 1819, and the years following witnessed his service as a missionary in Ohio, Michigan, and Illinois. But the organized response of the Church was long delayed, so long that in these crucial years when the proportionate strength of the Protestant Churches was assuming a fixed form in America, the Episcopalians lost an opportunity to rank with the larger bodies.

It was not wholly spiritual lethargy that accounted for the tardiness of the Church in throwing its resources into the West. Anglicanism, with its prescribed liturgical services and rigid tradition of ordered worship, its requirement of long years of training for the clergy, and its identification with cultural patterns that were non-existent in the western settlements, lacked the flexibility of adjustment necessary in the frontier scene. Moreover, the machinery of administration in the Episcopal Church proved too cumbersome to deal speedily with the new situation. Missionary areas had to be explored, districts for episcopal supervision created, bishops found and consecrated to exercise pastoral charge and jurisdiction in them, and men recruited for the evangelistic task. In brief, there was demanded of the Episcopal Church the kind of imaginative experiment and adaptation to local conditions which tested its claim to catholicity. Could Anglicanism take root in areas where the cultural traditions and historic patterns of religious thought that had always formed its background were not present?

The answer was given by the missionary activity of the Episcopal Church in the years before the Civil War. Tardily, but none the less surely, Anglicanism spread through the West. By 1835 the General Convention had made it plain that the missionary work of the Church was not to be the concern of special societies, but rather the opportunity and responsibility of every churchman. In that year a long and distinguished line of missionary bishops was started with the work of Jackson Kemper in the Northwest. Others followed: Talbot in Kemper's steps, Whipple in Minnesota, Freeman in the Southwest, Polk in Louisiana, Scott in Oregon, and Kip in California.

Simultaneously, the overseas activity of the Episcopal Church began. Missionaries went out to what is now the Missionary District of Liberia in 1836, a bishop being consecrated for that area fifteen years later. Henry Lockwood and Francis Hanson reached China in 1835. In 1844 William Boone was made bishop in the Chinese mission, a work later growing into the three American districts incorporated in the autonomous *Chung Hua Sheng Kung Hui*. Bishop Channing Moore Williams was given supervision over Japan in 1866, though direct evangelism was impossible in that country until the edicts against Christianity were withdrawn. There, as in China, the missionary districts of the American Episcopal Church later formed an important part of the independent Japanese Church of the Anglican Communion.

Thus the overseas mission of the Episcopal Church has steadily expanded, in increasingly close coöperation with the missionary extension of the other autonomous Anglican Churches. By the end of the nineteenth century, or shortly after, missionary districts had been formed in the Philippine Islands, Alaska, Brazil, and in those areas of Central America and the West Indies where the Church of England was not already at work. In the Hawaiian Islands, annexation by the United States caused the Anglican Church to hand over its flourishing mission to the care of the American Episcopal Church. Though World War II wrought havoc in the mission fields of Asia and the Pacific Islands, halting temporarily the work of evangelism and destroying a large part of the Church's material resources, yet today the missionary effort in those areas has been renewed with redoubled vigor.

### THE ANGLICAN CATHOLIC REVIVAL

THE significant influence in the life of eighteenth-century Anglicanism was that of the Evangelical Movement; in the nineteenth century it was that of the *Catholic Revival*.

By the middle of the nineteenth century the Evangelical Movement had passed the peak of its power in the life of the Church of England. Though continuing to inspire Anglican missionary and philanthropic activity, and still exercising compelling influence upon the religion of individuals, the Evangelical Movement offered no adequate answer to the new questions with which a revolutionary age faced the Church.

The ascendency of secularism and the consequent adjustment of Christianity to a subordinate position in men's lives bequeathed to the post-Reformation world the task of finding answers to some ultimate questions: What is the true nature of the Church? What is its relation to the State? To man's organized social and civic life? In the eighteenth century men were satisfied by shallow answers, largely because the crucial import of such questions was not perceived. The *laissez-faire* spiritual temper of the Establishment ignored the challenge of rationalism; the Evangelicals, concerned with a renewed personal devotion that expressed itself largely in terms of moral advance and philanthropic endeavor, gave the ultimate questions little thought.

With the last years of the eighteenth century, it was the disturbing impact of the Age of Revolution which uncovered these deep issues. Violent changes in the social and political order drove men to examine the very foundations of human society. This involved the thoughtful Christian in the doctrine of the Church. What was the character of the various memberships, social, political, and economic, that made up the tapestry of human community? How were these memberships related to each other? To what extent were their claims absolute? How were they to be related to man's supreme membership, his life in the community of Jesus Christ? Were these not, after all, the final questions for the Christian in this world?

In 1833 a small group of Oxford scholars challenged the Church of England with its responsibility for answering these questions out of its own historic theological tradition. With the publication of an arousing series of *Tracts for the Times,* John Henry Newman, Vicar of St. Mary's, Oxford, Edward Bouverie Pusey, Professor of Hebrew in the University, and the saintly John Keble, Vicar of Hursley, sought to make it clear that the Church of England could provide answers within the framework of a long-ignored heritage of Catholic theology. The Church, they maintained, was the Divine Society, autonomous in its life, absolute in its claims upon men, standing over against the world to proclaim man's salvation through his membership in the abiding community of Jesus Christ. Moreover, when the Church was true to its own nature, its claims were made apparent in those continuing Catholic institutions of the ages that shaped and expressed the very life of the Church. Hence the concern of the Tractarians with the authority with which the Saviour had endowed His Church, with the essentially sacramental character of its corporate life, and with the divine ministerial commission, transmitted from generation to generation by apostolic succession through the episcopate, and upon which the continuing life of the Catholic Church depends.

In brief, the purpose of the *Tracts* was to reawaken the Church of England to the implications of that basic Catholic heritage which Englishmen had refused to repudiate at the time of the Reformation. With this theological emphasis, the aim of the early leaders of the Oxford Movement was an intellectual one. Today their answers to these questions may not be wholly satisfactory, but it is plainly evident that they recognized the fundamental theological problems with which the modern age has confronted the Church. That recognition largely accounts for the enormous influence of the Oxford Movement throughout the Anglican Communion in the past hundred years.

## THE IMPACT OF THE OXFORD MOVEMENT

THE impact of the Oxford Movement was not confined to the Church of England. All through the Anglican Communion different aspects of the · Church's life felt its quickening and invigorating influence. As early as 1842, Bishop Denison of Salisbury acknowledged that however much he disapproved certain features of the movement, it must be recognized that under its influence the standards of discipline, faithfulness, and personal holiness among the clergy had been raised, the sacraments restored to their centrality in the life of the Church as instruments of the operation of divine grace, and the study of theology made once more the primary concern of the mind of the Church.

Over the years that followed, it became evident that Denison had not exaggerated the importance of the Anglican Catholic Revival. The effects of the Oxford Movement were seen in every area of the life of the English Church and its sister-churches overseas. Anglican spiritual life found new depths with the recovery of those ancient treasures of Catholic devotion which belong to the Church Universal. Intellectually, a heroic attempt was made to set forward the Catholicism of the Christian tradition in its broadest and most challenging forms. A long line of distinguished theologians rose to relate the Catholic faith to the conditions that surrounded man in the modern world. Moreover, the Oxford Movement displayed a social and moral conscience akin to that of the Evangelical Revival. Few stories of spiritual heroism are more thrilling than those written in the sacrificial labors of hundreds of clergy who sought to express the pastoral ideals of the movement in their care for the neglected folk of the crowded city slums and the remote rural areas.

Today the Oxford Movement is no longer identifiable as a separate stream of thought and activity within Anglicanism. Precisely as was true of the Evangelical Movement the Catholic Revival recalled Anglicans to forgotten aspects of their own heritage and tradition, and over the years its permanent values are seen in the greater richness of the ethos of Anglicanism itself.

Often in any strong religious movement, the best advocates of the real nature of the revival are not its vociferous extremists. This had been true in the Evangelical Movement when evangelical churchmen found it difficult to prevent their friends, less devoted to the principles of the Church of England, from joining the dissenting churches. A similar situation arose in the course of the Oxford Movement. Fear that this new emphasis would lead Anglicans to Roman Catholicism, an attitude that seemed justified by the defection of Newman and others, was engendered largely by the activities of shallow extremists. When events proved this fear to be without foundation, it was replaced by the equally strong suspicion that this movement would repudiate the Reformation heritage of the English Church and bring the narrow doctrinal and authoritarian principles of Romanism into

Anglican Church life and thought. The recovery of the beauty of the Church's worship in the external forms of ceremonies, vestments, and music, the revival of the monastic life for men and women in the Anglican Communion, the emphasis upon the ancient doctrines, discipline, and devotional practices of the Church—all these provoked bitter controversy, the vestiges of which still linger in the Anglican Churches.

The unfortunate aspect of this controversy was to set in false opposition the positions labeled "High Church" and "Low Church." Even worse, perhaps, was the investing of those terms of great Christian significance, *Catholic* and *Evangelical,* with narrow and partisan meaning. Today it is clear that what was at issue underneath this tension was the claim of Anglicanism to a kind of Catholicism, unfettered by the authoritarian rigidity and medieval dogmatism of Rome, that was truly part of the Reformation heritage of the Church of England. Earlier, evangelicalism had struggled to find its rightful expression in the fulness of the Christian tradition which Anglicanism strove to maintain. Now the integrity of truly Catholic experience and life within that ethos was displayed.

In one sense this controversy of a generation or two ago has played an important part in the history of Anglican thought. It has brought to the churches of the Anglican Communion a greater knowledge and more sympathetic understanding of other Christian traditions. It has led Anglicans to a deeper apprehension of the unique values of their own heritage, where at best, truth is seen to lie in the inseparable conjunction of the things Catholic and the things Evangelical.

## POST-REFORMATION ROMAN CATHOLICISM

As a result of the Counter-Reformation revival in the sixteenth century, the Roman Church enjoyed nearly a century of prestige and achievement. Reinvigorated by reform and renewed devotion, papal Catholicism launched a vigorous and diverse program of education and evangelism, directed toward the faithful Catholics as well as to the recovery of ground lost to Protestantism. These forces spent themselves, however, with the gradual ascendency of secularism in the modern world. In the long run, the permanent results of the Counter-Reformation were those which found concrete expression in the canons and decrees of Trent. It was the new dogmatic rigidity and the narrowness of temper that so sharply differentiated modern Romanism from medieval Catholicism.

This aspect of reformed Rome was manifested repeatedly in the seventeenth and eighteenth centuries, perhaps never with more tragic results than in the famous Jansenist controversy. Cornelius Jansen, a Dutchman of earnest devotion and austere piety, the leader of a small group of like-minded Catholic scholars at the University of Louvain, turned from the theology of the medieval scholastics to reassert the primacy of the patristic literature of the Early Church. Much affected by those writings of St. Augustine which emphasized not only the initiative of God in human salvation, but also the continual dependence of man upon the divine mercy, Jansen attacked the prevailing semi-Pelagian doctrines. To him the laxity of Jesuit moral theology was dangerous to souls; the easy path to salvation by pious works of outward observance was a parody of true Catholic doctrine.

Jansenism was a kind of evangelical Catholicism, not a little affected by Calvinism, and reflecting in its emphasis upon intense personal religion similar spiritual forces to those which stirred the Protestant world in the Pietist awakening. Finding its most vigorous champions in France, Jansenism centered in the Abbey of Port Royal near Versailles. There the theological controversy raged in the middle of the seventeenth century, the most notable incident being the devastating indictment of the Jesuits by Blaise Pascal in the memorable *Provincial Letters*. But Jansenism represented a spirit for which there was no room in the new Romanism. Repeated papal condemnations reinforced the opposition of the Jesuit order; Louis XIV, near the end of his reign, sealed the fate of Jansenism in France by placing the power of his government behind the forces of repression. The Abbey of Port Royal was destroyed, and the original spirit of the Jansenist movement was crushed. Jansenism survived only as a cover for a minority group of political and ecclesiastical malcontents.

The tragic consequence of the inability of post-Tridentine Romanism to absorb the evangelical values of Jansenism was the spiritual impoverishment of the French Church in the days of the *ancien régime*. With Jansenism branded as heresy and Huguenot Protestantism under severe persecution, Frenchmen had only the choice between the skepticism of Voltaire and the decadent Catholicism of the Jesuits. No small part of the violence suffered by the Church during the French Revolution was rooted in these repressive activities of the early eighteenth century.

## PAPALISM AND MODERN ROME

THE inner history of Roman Catholicism in the centuries since the Reformation is largely the story of two interesting movements of thought within the Roman Church, movements having great significance for the Christian world of which Roman Catholics form such a large part. The first concerns the papal claim to temporal sovereignty, a claim successfully exercised within the framework of the theocratic Medieval Commonwealth during the period when the power of the papacy was at its height. The second is the belief in papal infallibility, a doctrine which received dogmatic definition at the Vatican Council of 1870.

The claim of the popes to temporal sovereignty stretches back to the formation of Medieval Europe after the collapse of the Roman Empire. When the papacy emerged as the stabilizing center of the new Christian Commonwealth, it was possessed of endowments of feudal estates and properties, largely situated in central Italy. These became the nucleus of the Papal States over which the popes presently ruled as temporal princes. Throughout the Middle Ages the foreign policy of the papal chancellery was directed to the extension of this temporal power by reducing, wherever possible, the political units of Medieval Europe to feudal obedience to the pope. At the same time, and indeed, long after feudal Europe had vanished in the changes of the Renaissance, the papacy could permit no strong power to secure a foothold in the Italian peninsula, lest the papal principality be deprived of its independence and the popes stripped of actual temporal authority.

Behind this determination to preserve the real exercise of sovereign temporal rule lay the medieval theory of the plenitude of power residing in the pope as Vicar of Christ. All power is given of God, and that which is called temporal (the authority of the State) is secondary to and derivative from that which is spiritual (the authority of the Church). To use the words of Pope Boniface VIII, by whom the classic exposition of this theory was made in the end of the Middle Ages, "Both are in the power of the Church, both the spiritual and the temporal swords . . . the temporal authority ought to be subject to the spiritual power." However it might be explained that spiritual power is vested in the papacy directly, and temporal authority only indirectly, the subordinate character of the latter provides a theory upon which the papal claim to universal dominion rests.

The existence of the independent Papal States presented to men an actualization of this theory, on a small scale but none the less significant. Driven again and again in the modern world to come to terms with the new omnicompetent states, Roman Catholicism shelved its medieval theories of power, though it did not repudiate them. Challenged by the absolutism of the Catholic monarchies of the eighteenth century, and confronted later by the rigid principles of the separation of Church and State that characterized the democracies, it was inexpedient to proclaim the old pretensions to universal dominion. Yet as long as the Papal States existed, the principles underlying the ancient theory were in actual operation.

Thus we understand better the stubborn papal resistance to the Italian *risorgimento* of the nineteenth century, the nationalist movement for the unification of Italy. When the Papal States were seized by the troops of Victor Emmanuel of Savoy and Rome made the capital of the new kingdom of Italy, Pius IX shut himself into the Vatican, refusing to acknowledge the loss of temporal power. There the popes remained, "prisoners of the Vatican," despite the conciliatory overtures of the Italian monarchy, until the concordat of 1929 between Pius XI and the fascist government of Mussolini. By that agreement the temporal sovereignty of the papacy was restored. In the miniature sovereign state of the Vatican City the principles underlying the theory of the plenitude of power are once more in operation.

Though perhaps based upon concepts of power which belong to the Middle Ages, Roman Catholicism has still a well-defined theory of the relation of Church and State. In the modern political and ideological chaos more than a little of the increasing strength of Romanism is due to the authoritative appeal that such a doctrine presents. Equally, the claim to speak decisively and infallibly in the theological confusion of today's world provides for many the kind of authority to which men are tempted to submit in an insecure and fearful age.

The doctrine of papal infallibility is the natural outcome of the belief in papal supremacy. The procedure of the sixteenth-century Council of Trent made it clear that for Roman Catholicism the papacy was the sole agency by which the mind of the Church on theological and moral issues was to be declared. This concept of supremacy, which made the papal institution the guardian and interpreter of all truth necessary for man's salvation, logically involved a definition in terms of infallibility. By erecting an authoritative institution through which Christian truth is rightly made known, Roman Catholicism found it an intellectual and moral necessity that such an agency be clothed with infallibility. Given the acceptance of an institution of this character in Christianity, anything less than this spiritual endowment would be intolerable.

All through the eighteenth and early nineteenth centuries the tide ran strongly toward the definition of infallibility, hastened by the opposition to secularism and influenced by the reactionary forces with which Rome aligned itself in the Age of Revolution. Papal bulls and decrees assumed an infallible tone; the group of European Catholics who clung to the older notions of conciliar supremacy found themselves an ever-dwindling minority.

The definition of infallibility came at the Vatican Council in 1870, where it was proclaimed that "the Roman Pontiff, when he speaks *ex cathedra* (that is, when, fulfilling the office of pastor and teacher of all Christians, on his supreme apostolical authority, he defines a doctrine concerning faith or morals to be held by the Universal Church) . . . is endowed with that infallibility with which the Divine Redeemer has willed that His Church . . . should be equipped. . . ." And making it clear that the ancient concepts of the supremacy of the General Council in Christendom are no longer tenable, the decree continues, "Such definitions of the Roman Pontiff are of themselves, and not by virtue of the consent of the Church, irreformable."

Those who protested against the infallibility decree were

a distinguished few, numbering among them some of the foremost Catholic scholars and historians in Europe, but their warning voices went unheeded. Papalism had come to its complete triumph in modern Romanism. An answer to the problem of authority had been found, but it is difficult to see that the sacrifices involved were justified, except on the assumption that the one essential institution of the Christian Church is the Roman papacy. Today between Rome and the rest of Christendom yawns the apparently unbridgeable chasm of the infallible *magisterium* of the pope.

## OLD CATHOLICISM

OPPOSITION to the drift toward infallibility, though confined to minority groups within Roman Catholicism, was continuous during the seventeenth and eighteenth centuries. The most impressive witness against the growth of papalism was that made by French Catholics in the movement known as *Gallicanism*. Originating in the ancient claims of the Church in France to enjoy special rights and privileges within the framework of papal Catholicism, and supported by the concept of the independence of national Churches, Gallicanism asserted itself vigorously against the increased exercise of papal supremacy after the Council of Trent. On several occasions it seemed as though outbursts of Gallican feeling might lead France to break with Rome as England had done earlier, but the time for such violent action had passed. Gallicanism was too doctrinaire to arouse the entire nation, and the Bourbon government of the eighteenth century, unable to risk alienating the papacy, kept the Gallican spirit in check.

A corresponding movement of anti-papal character broke out in the imperial territories in the days of the Empress Maria Teresa and her son, Joseph II. Nicholas von Hontheim and other German and Austrian bishops attempted to halt the drift toward the papal assumption of that jurisdiction and authority which for centuries had been thought to be inherently lodged in the episcopate of the Church. *Febronianism* (von Hontheim wrote under the pen-name "Febronius") like extreme Gallicanism, revived the old ideas of the supremacy of a General Council, and the honorific character of the papal primacy. But Febronianism could not survive the impact of the Age of Revolution. Catholic forces everywhere were identifying themselves with the reaction against liberalism that swept Europe in the early nineteenth century, and the alliance between Rome and the Hapsburg monarchy after the Congress of Vienna brought an end to any lingering Febronian activity.

Today movements such as Gallicanism and Febronianism are of interest only to the historian. The spirit animating them was completely smothered by the ultramontane landslide of 1870. Nevertheless, they serve to remind us that the Catholicism which the Anglican tradition proclaims is not a curious freak of ecclesiastical history. The principles on which the Anglican position rests were at work in Catholic thought in many centuries and in many areas of the Church's life.

A number of Catholics who could not in conscience yield these principles in the face of the infallibility decree of 1870, broke with Rome, loyal to what they called *Old*

*Catholicism.* Groups in Germany, Switzerland, and other portions of central Europe, formed themselves into Churches, retaining much of the ancient faith and practice of Catholicism, but rejecting the new papalism. In the process of organization they turned for assistance to the Church of Utrecht in Holland, a small body of Catholics who had separated from the papal Church in the days of the Jansenist controversy. The new separatists received episcopal orders from these Dutch Old Catholics, among whom the line of succession in the episcopate had been preserved. They were thus enabled to take a place among the non-Roman bodies of Catholic Christendom.

The Old Catholic Communion today is composed of a number of small self-governing Churches in Europe, bearing witness to the vitality of the broadest Catholic principles. They are united in the bonds of a common faith and practice, and are in communion with the Archbishop and ancient see of Utrecht. Their general ecclesiastical organization and theological position have many points of kinship with Anglican Churches. In the United States the Old Catholic fellowship is represented by the Polish National Catholic Church, while in the Philippine Islands the Philippine Independent Church, though not a member-church of the Old Catholic Communion, is nevertheless a similar body, being the Church of several million Filipinos who maintain their traditional Catholic faith and practice without allegiance to Rome.

Friendly relations between Anglicans and Old Catholics, which existed from the formation of Old Catholicism, have culminated in full communion between the two Churches. In the Bonn Agreement of 1931 each Church recognized "the catholicity and independence of the other," and agreed "to admit members of the other Communion to participate in the Sacraments." In the United States the Episcopal Church enjoys this sacramental relation with the Polish National Catholic Church, and a similar concordat of full communion has been established between Episcopalians and members of the Philippine Independent Church.

## THE EASTERN ORTHODOX CHURCH

THE final separation between Eastern and Western Christianity came in the dispute between the Roman pope and the Patriarch of Constantinople in 1054. In the subsequent centuries few earnest attempts were made to heal the schism. On the contrary, the breach was widened by the increasing cultural and political differences between East and West, a situation that became obvious in the years of the Crusades. The unhappy experiences of the Eastern Empire with the European Crusaders, whose political designs in the Near East often over-rode their religious fervor to rescue the Holy Land from the infidel, heightened the tensions between western Europe and Byzantium. Thus in the last centuries of the Middle Ages, the Eastern Empire, clinging precariously to but a fragment of the vast territory once under Greek rule, found itself facing the onslaught of the Mohammedan Turks single-handed, isolated from the rest of Christian Europe.

With the fall of Constantinople in 1453 the thousand-year-old Byzantine Christian empire was swept away. The Turkish conquerors turned the famous Cathedral of St. Sophia into a mosque, and brought the Greek Orthodox Church under strict governmental supervision. Christians speedily became a despised alien minority in the Turkish

Empire. They were exploited economically, subjected to political and social discrimination, and every pressure was brought on them to accept the religion of Islam.

Though the organization of the Orthodox Church was suffered to exist and the patriarchate preserved, it was largely as a means through which the sultan, controlling the appointment of patriarchs, could control his Christian subjects. In these circumstances the condition of the Church was one of spiritual decay, often deliberately fostered by the Turkish government. Not until the Balkan States, in which the great majority of Orthodox Christians lived, won their independence from the Ottoman power in the nineteenth century, did the Greek Orthodox Church finds its opportunity for spiritual independence and recovery.

The present divisions of Eastern Christendom reflect the tortuous path of the history of the Near East in the past thousand years. The ancient Orthodox Patriarchates of Constantinople, Alexandria, Antioch, and Jerusalem still exist, but their direct jurisdiction is limited to the small minority of Christians in the Islamic lands where they are located. The Orthodox Churches of the Balkan States, in which Christians form the greater number of the inhabitants, are now autocephalous—that is, while linked with Constantinople with ties of history and traditional respect, they are actually self-governing and independent national Churches. The unity of faith, worship, and order which binds these Churches into one Communion of Eastern Orthodoxy is not unlike the kind of unity that is found in the independent Churches of the Anglican Communion.

Side by side with these Orthodox Churches are the Separated or *Oriental* Churches, remnants for the most part of the Nestorian and Monophysite bodies which were formed after the divisive theological controversies of the fifth century. The Coptic Church of Egypt, the Ethiopian Church of Abyssinia, the Armenian Church, and the Syrian Jacobite Church all fall into this group. While in some cases they are numerically of no significance, yet in others they outnumber the Orthodox Eastern Christians in the areas where they are situated.

The theological issues, intensified by the related nationalist movements in the ancient Byzantine Empire, over which these Churches separated themselves from the Patriarchate of Constantinople, are now no longer acute. The differences are generally agreed to be only terminological, matters of the precise theological definition of the nature and person of Christ rather than any fundamental disagreement over the meaning of the Incarnation. Today there is a new hope that Eastern Christendom as a whole is moving toward a unity which it has not known for centuries. But unfortunately, both the Orthodox and the Oriental Churches, strongly nationalist in character and identified very closely with different racial and cultural scenes, find great difficulties in any effective unity of organization. One of the greatest needs of Christendom is for the Eastern Churches to make their rightful contribution out of their ancient tradition of Christian life and thought.

Roman Catholicism has made its own inroads into Eastern Christianity. Since the days of the Crusades small groups of Eastern Christians have been induced to give their allegiance to Rome. In the sixteenth and seventeenth centuries the number of these Uniate Churches was increased, and today there are bodies of this type broken from nearly all the different Eastern Churches. Simply stated, the *uniate* principle allows the Easterners to retain their distinctive liturgical rites and disciplinary customs in return for obedience to papal authority. The end result, however, appears to be absorption into the rigid system of Roman Catholicism, for local independence tends to disappear in the face of the stronger and more clearly defined discipline of Rome. Recently, political factors have invaded this realm of ecclesiastical loyalties. In 1946 the largest uniate group, the Ruthenians, transferred their obedience from Rome to the Patriarchate of Moscow, apparently under considerable pressure from the Soviet government. The events surrounding this repudiation of uniate status by nearly four million Christians in central Europe are still obscure. All that is evident is the wide increase of the ecclesiastical jurisdiction of the Russian Orthodox Patriarchate in those areas of Europe dominated by the Soviet political power.

## THE MOSCOW PATRIARCHATE

THE Russian Patriarchate deserves special attention today, if only because the Orthodox Christians subject to the spiritual rule of Moscow constitute one of the largest groups in the Eastern Church. After Constantinople fell to the Turks and the ancient Eastern Empire disappeared, Ivan IV of Russia assumed the title of Tsar and the style of the Byzantine Caesars, the theory being that an Orthodox Christian Emperor must still reign somewhere. Moscow became the holy city, the "Third Rome." The correlative assumption was that Moscow had inherited the spiritual leadership of Orthodoxy formerly belonging to Constantinople. This theory was given expression in the last years of the sixteenth century when the Russian Church was recognized as a separate patriarchate of Eastern Orthodoxy.

In one respect, at least, Moscow emulated ancient Byzantium. A strict imperial control was exerted over the life and thought of the Church. Caesaropapism was even more characteristic of the Russian Tsars than it had been of the Eastern emperors in the Middle Ages. Peter the Great, perhaps affected by the western influences with which he sought to make Russia a European country, went so far in the direction of imperial control of the Church as to abolish the patriarchate itself. Under his reforms, the powers of the patriarch were exercised by the Holy Synod, a kind of central ecclesiastical committee, the dominant figure in which was the Tsar's deputy. The Russian Church was thus virtually reduced to a department of State, stripped of all power of self-reform and reinvigoration, becoming just one more agency of government in the Tsarist absolute State. For two centuries the Church remained paralyzed by this subordination to the imperial rule, and it is not surprising that the Bolshevik revolutionaries of 1917–18 viewed the Church as completely identified with the reactionary government which they sought to overthrow.

The victory of the revolution was the defeat of both Church and Tsarist government in Russia. The Bolsheviks and their Soviet successors attacked the Church without mercy, destroying its institutions, confiscating its wealth and properties, and sending thousands of priests and monks to death or slavery in the labor camps of the Siberian wastes. Violent persecution of Christianity was succeeded by years of discrimination against Christians, and the imposition of such disabilities upon those who sought to practice their religion that for a time it looked as though the Church would disappear with the death of the older generation. But Christianity proved to be more stubbornly intrenched than the revolutionary government had believed. The long years of privation and economic distress, during which a communist government that had promised the utopian plenty of an economic democracy became more and more like its tyrannous Tsarist predecessor, drove the masses of folk to what no one could take from them: their faith in God. The sudden plunge into the horrors of World War II completed this return to religion on the part of great masses of Russian people.

The Soviet government today grants recognition to the Russian Church, having allowed the restoration of the patriarchate in 1943. The control of the Church by the government is as strict as it was in the days of the Tsars, but there is one important difference. Political control today is that of a frankly godless government, without the paralyzing doctrine of the sacred powers of an Orthodox Caesar to hold the Church in submission as long as that theory is maintained. However much the Russian Church is made an instrument of the Soviet political power, it is not identified with that government in the same fashion in which it was linked with the Tsarist regime.

## PROTESTANTISM TODAY

ONE of the most encouraging manifestations of Christian spiritual power is the reawakening that has marked the Protestant world since the last war. Everywhere there has been a recognition that purely humanistic idealism is insufficient for the rebuilding of man's common life. On all sides there has been a rediscovery and new appropriation of the ultimate Christian principles upon which alone human society can be securely grounded.

This has brought a new understanding of the relevance of the Christian faith to the problems of our time, and has found expression in a variety of areas of Christian thought and activity. Protestant theology, for example, has been marked by a vigorous return to orthodoxy. In some circles this has taken the form of a new emphasis upon the classic doctrines of Reformation Protestantism; in others the theological revival has resulted in a new understanding of those basic elements of the Christian tradition that are common to Catholic and Protestant thought alike. The significance of this revival lies in its return to the biblical doctrines of man and his relation to God. Once again the mind of Christendom perceives more clearly the meaning of the redemptive activity of God in Jesus Christ and its continuous impact upon human life and institutions.

Accompanying this activity has been the widespread renewal of concern with the nature of Christian worship and the full participation of the Christian community, lay and clerical alike, in it. The *Liturgical Movement,* as it is called, has captured the attention of Catholics and Protestants alike. Among Roman Catholics wider and more informed participation of the laity in the Mass is sought, and experiments in the use of vernacular language are being made. Protestant Churches are rediscovering the Christian heritage of corporate and liturgical worship that was neglected by many groups after the Reformation. Christians of all allegiances are finding their commitment to Jesus Christ strengthened and empowered by a new involvement in the Church's sacramental and liturgical worship.

## THE CHALLENGE OF DIVIDED CHRISTENDOM

PERHAPS the most dramatic manifestation of the new spirit in Protestantism—and it is by no means absent from the Catholic Churches—is the response to the challenge presented to the Churches by the scandal of divided Christendom. During the last fifty years there has been a remarkable growth of concern for the restoration of the unity of Christendom, expressed not only in the desire for closer cooperation in many areas of Christian work and witness, but also in the determination to strive for the achievement of organic unity—the healing of the divisions that at present mark Christendom. This *Ecumenical Movement* has already resulted in a wide and sympathetic understanding of each other among Christians of all Churches. In some cases, actual unions have been achieved among Protestant bodies, bringing together groups which have been long separated from one another. A half-century ago Christian reunion was regarded as the ecclesiastical fad of a few, or at best the dream of visionaries; today it is the earnest spiritual concern of many thousands.

The gains of the Ecumenical Movement have come

slowly. Years have been spent in patient study and discussion of honest differences, while the search for a better understanding of our separations and the ways to overcome them still continues in constant ecumenical exploration. Four centuries of division lie behind Western Christianity today. Even older divisions separate West and East. Yet the progress made in a few decades has been remarkable, and unmistakably under the guiding power of the Holy Spirit. The world-wide conferences on faith and order, begun at Lausanne in 1927 and continuing ever since in one form or another, have provided Christendom with a thrilling witness to the unifying power of the Lord in His Church. Today the work of such conferences, together with that of many other ecumenical gatherings devoted to the study of Christian life and work, has been given direction by the World Council of Churches. From Geneva, where the World Council maintains its permanent headquarters, has come guidance and encouragement of ecumenical activities throughout the entire world.[4]

There are immense difficulties still before the Ecumenical Movement, yet the evident stirrings of heart and mind everywhere in Christendom are full of promise. The Churches of Eastern Orthodoxy are still unable to make their important contribution to the recovery of the wholeness of Christendom, partly because there are internal divisions among Eastern Churches which impede their activity, and partly because political conditions in central

---

[4] The participation of the Episcopal Church in the Ecumenical Movement is briefly summarized in Volume VI of this series, *The Episcopal Church and Its Work* (Revised Edition, 1961), pages 262-276.

and eastern Europe still restrict the Churches there from their full Christian activity. On the other hand, the Roman Catholic Church, which for many years took no part in the general ecumenical activity, has more recently shown a sympathetic attitude to the problems of Christian division. Today Roman Catholics have a new sensitivity towards the difficulties that lie in the path of Christian unity, and ecumenical discussion between Catholics and Protestants has been encouraged by the Roman Church. However distant may be the fulfillment of the hope that an ecumenical bridge might some day span the deepest chasm that divides Christendom, yet it is not an accomplishment to be regarded as beyond the power of the one God and Father of us all. No world-wide movement for Church unity can achieve more than a partial approximation to the will of the Lord without the active cooperation of the Roman Church. As the Lambeth Conference of Anglican bishops has asserted, ". . . there can be no fulfillment of the Divine purpose in any scheme of reunion which does not ultimately include the great Latin Church of the West, with which our history has been so closely associated in the past, and to which we are still bound by so many ties of common faith and tradition."

But the recognition of difficulties has never paralyzed Christian efforts of any kind. On the contrary, as the whole sweep of the history of the Church reveals, the greatest vitality of the Christian spirit is most often displayed in the face of the greatest difficulties. It may be so with the Ecumenical Movement in the years ahead.

THE story of the Christian Church has no end. We have reached that page of Christian history on which contemporary events are being recorded. To conclude here is but to pause on the threshold of tomorrow, but we know that contemporary events will find their meaning in the totality of Christian experience that we have witnessed through the ages. Everywhere in the course of Church history one thing stands out with compelling clarity. It is the ever-renewed vitality of that ultimate human community which reflects the reality of the *City of God*. History for the Christian points beyond time to the Author and Finisher of all things. The life of the Christian fellowship continues to be central in what man calls history because it continues to be both the scene and the means of God's redemptive activity in the world of His creation.

# About the Author

THE REV. POWEL MILLS DAWLEY, PH.D., D.D., is Professor of Ecclesiastical History and Sub-Dean at the General Theological Seminary. He was formerly Associate Rector of St. David's Church, Baltimore, and Dean of St. Luke's Cathedral, Portland, Maine. A graduate of Brown University and the Episcopal Theological School, he received his Ph.D. from the University of Cambridge, England. He is co-author of *The Religion of the Prayer Book*, and author of *The Words of Life; John Whitgift and the Reformation* (The Hale Lectures for 1953); *Our Christian Heritage*; and *The Episcopal Church and Its Work*, Volume VI in THE CHURCH'S TEACHING.

OTHERS WHO WERE MEMBERS OF THE AUTHORS' COMMITTEE AT THE TIME THIS BOOK WAS PUBLISHED IN ITS FIRST EDITION

THE REV. STANLEY BROWN-SERMAN, D.D., the late Dean and Professor of New Testament Language and Literature at the Protestant Episcopal Seminary in Virginia.

THE REV. ROBERT CLAUDE DENTAN, PH.D., Professor of Old Testament Literature and Interpretation at the General Theological Seminary and author of Volume I in THE CHURCH'S TEACHING, *The Holy Scriptures*.

THE REV. JOHN HEUSS, D.D., Rector of Trinity Church, New York, and co-chairman of the Authors' Committee.

THE RT. REV. ARTHUR C. LICHTENBERGER, D.D., Presiding Bishop.

THE REV. C. KILMER MYERS, S.T.D., Director, Urban Training Center, Chicago, Ill.

THE RT. REV. JAMES A. PIKE, J.S.D., Bishop of California, and co-author of Volume III in THE CHURCH'S TEACHING, *The Faith of the Church*.

THE REV. W. NORMAN PITTENGER, S.T.D., Professor of Apologetics at the General Theological Seminary, and co-author of Volume III in THE CHURCH'S TEACHING, *The Faith of the Church.*

THE REV. FREDERICK Q. SHAFER, Professor of Religion and Chaplain at Bard College.

THE REV. CHARLES W. F. SMITH, D.D., Professor of the Literature and Interpretation of the New Testament at the Episcopal Theological School.

THE REV. VESPER O. WARD, D.D., formerly Professor of Christian Education and Homiletics at the School of Theology, the University of the South.

THE REV. THEODORE O. WEDEL, PH.D., formerly Warden of the College of Preachers, Washington, D. C.

# Books for Reference

BIBLIOGRAPHIES of Church history for specialists and advanced students are readily available, and the books listed here are not intended as such. This list has been compiled for use by parish clergy, Church teachers, and lay leaders as an aid to their teaching responsibilities, and for popular reading by Church people who wish to know more about the history of Christianity. The books listed provide greater detail of events, background, and personalities than space has permitted in this volume. In nearly every case the books are suitable for the general reader. Paperback titles are listed with an asterisk.

## SURVEYS OF CHURCH HISTORY

The following are standard one-volume textbooks of the history of the Church:

*A History of the Christian Church* by Williston Walker (New York: Scribner. Revised and Enlarged. 1959). In long use as a student's text.

*A History of Christianity* by Kenneth S. Latourette (New York: Harper. 1953). Very readable full treatment.

*The Christian Society* by Stephen Neill (London: Nisbet. 1952). An admirable survey.

*A History of the Christian Church* by Lars P. Qualben (New York: Thomas Nelson & Sons. Revised and Enlarged. 1938).

*Documents of the Christian Church,* ed. by Henry Bettenson (New York: Oxford. 1943). An extremely valuable collection of brief selections from the chief documents and source materials of Christian history.

The following books deal more briefly with the whole sweep of Church history:

*Christianity* by S. C. Carpenter (London: Penguin Books. 1953). A thoughtful introduction.

*A Short History of Our Religion* by D. C. Somervell (London: Bell. 1936). Excellent.

*Militant in Earth* by Edward R. Hardy, Jr. (New York: Oxford. 1940). The mission of the Church through the ages.

*The Church of Our Fathers* by Roland Bainton (New York: Scribner. 1948). Introductory and excellent for younger readers.

*Ye Are the Body* by Bonnell Spencer (West Park, New York: Holy Cross Press. 1950). An admirable short history.

*The Divine Commission* by Frank E. Wilson (New York: Morehouse-Barlow. 1940). Long a standard popular history.

## CHAPTER I: THE CHURCH AND THE ROMAN WORLD

GENERAL STUDIES OF THE EARLY CHURCH

*A History of the Early Church* by J. W. C. Wand (London: Methuen. 1937). A standard work.

*The Church in the Ancient World* by L. Elliott-Binns (London: Unicorn. 1938). A brief sketch, interestingly presented.

*The Early Church* by George Hodges (Boston: Houghton Mifflin. 1915). One of the best books on the Early Church for the general reader.

*Life in the Early Church A.D. 33-313* by A. E. Welsford (New York: Seabury. 1953). Readable and informative.

*Constantine and the Conversion of Europe* by A. H. M. Jones (London: Hodder & Stoughton. 1948). An excellent study.

*The Environment of Early Christianity* by Samuel Angus (New York: Scribner. 1915). The social and religious conditions of the Roman world.

*The Making of the Church* by J. G. Davies (London: Skeffington. 1960).

*A History of Early Christian Literature* by Edgar J. Goodspeed (Chicago: Chicago University Press. 1942). A helpful introduction.

*The Early Christian Fathers,* ed. Henry Bettenson (New York: Oxford. 1956). Brief selections from the writings of the Fathers.

*Handbook of the Early Christian Fathers* by B. Leigh-Bennett (London: Williams & Norgate). A simple treatment of the thought of the chief early Christian Fathers.

*The Latin Doctors* by J. W. C. Wand (New York: Morehouse-Barlow. 1948).

*The Greek Doctors* by J. W. C. Wand (New York: Morehouse-Barlow. 1949).

WORSHIP IN THE EARLY CHURCH

*Christian Worship* by T. S. Garrett (New York: Oxford. 1961). See the early chapters.

*The Lay Folks' History of the Liturgy* by E. Crewdson Thomas (London. Rivington. 1929). The first part deals with the Early Church.

*Early Christians at Prayer* by William E. Barnes (New York: Morehouse. 1925).

*The Prayer of the Early Christians* by Fernand Cabrol (New York: Benzinger. 1930).

*A History of Christian Worship* by Oscar Hardman (Nashville: Abingdon-Cokesbury. 1937). Treats the whole history of Christian worship.

*The Early History of the Liturgy* by J. H. Srawley (New York: Macmillan. Revised Edition. 1947). For more advanced readers.

OTHER ASPECTS OF EARLY CHURCH LIFE

*The Formation of the New Testament* by Edgar J. Goodspeed (Chicago: Chicago University Press. 1926).

*The Bible in the Church* by Robert McQueen Grant (New York: Macmillan. 1948).

* *The Desert Fathers* by Helen Waddell (London: Constable). The early Christian monks and hermits.

*In the Steps of St. Paul* by H. C. V. Morton (New York: Dodd Mead. 1936). A fascinating view of the Mediterranean world of St. Paul's travels.

*Acts of the Apostles* by A. W. F. Blunt in *The Clarendon Bible* (New York: Oxford. 1925). A useful commentary for teachers.

*Everyman's Book of Saints* by C. P. S. Clarke (New York: Morehouse. 1914).

\* *Faithful Witnesses,* ed. by Edward R. Hardy (New York: Association Press. 1959). Records of early Christian martyrs.

## CHAPTER II: THE MEDIEVAL COMMONWEALTH

GENERAL STUDIES OF THE MEDIEVAL CHURCH

*A History of the Medieval Church* by M. Deanesly (London: Methuen). A short history of the Church in the Middle Ages.

*A History of Medieval Europe* by R. H. C. Davis (New York: Longmans. 1957). A standard text, excellent on the Church.

\* *The Portable Medieval Reader,* ed. by J. B. Ross and M. M. McLaughlin (New York: Viking Press. 1946). Interesting readings on all aspects of medieval life and thought.

\* *Medieval Panorama* by G. G. Coulton (New York: Macmillan. 1938). Sketches of medieval life.

MEDIEVAL FAITH AND PRACTICE

*Church Services and Service Books before the Reformation* by Henry Barclay Swete (New York: Macmillan. 1930).

*The Lay Folks' History of the Liturgy* by E. Crewdson Thomas (London: Rivington. 1929).

*The Books of the Latin Liturgy* by Fernand Cabrol (St. Louis: Herder. 1932).

*The Home of the Monk* by D. H. S. Cranage (New York: Macmillan. 1926). An excellent study.

*The People's Faith in the Time of Wycliffe* by Bernard L. Manning (New York: Macmillan). A little volume dealing with popular religion.

*A Medieval Scrap-Heap* by William Edwards (London: Rivington. 1930). A collection of fascinating notes on the outlook and practices of medieval people.

*The Medieval Missionary* by James Thayer Addison (New York: International Missionary Council. 1936). The story of the conversion of barbarian Europe.

THE END OF THE MIDDLE AGES

*The Age of Schism* by Herbert Bruce (New York: Macmillan. 1907). An introductory survey of the period of the origins of the Reformation.

*Erasmus and the Northern Renaissance* by M. A. Phillips (London: Hodder & Stoughton. 1949).

*Renaissance and Reformation Times* by Dorothy Mills (New York: G. P. Putnam's Sons. 1939). A very useful school text, highly recommended.

## CHAPTER III: CHRISTIANITY IN ENGLAND

GENERAL HISTORIES OF THE CHURCH OF ENGLAND

*A History of the Church in England* by J. R. H. Moorman (London: A. & C. Black. 1953). The standard one-volume textbook.

*A Dictionary of English Church History,* ed. by S. L. Ollard and G. Crosse (London: Mowbray). Invaluable for reference.

*A History of Christianity in England* by E. O. James (London: Hutchinson's University Library. 1949). A short history.

*The English Religious Tradition* by Norman Sykes (London: SCM Press. 1953). Brief sketches.

*Christianity in England* by Cyril A. Alington (New York: Oxford. 1942).

THE CHURCH BEFORE THE NORMAN CONQUEST

*The Conversion of the English* by Huntly Curtois (New York: Macmillan. 1927). The early years of Christianity in England.

*Ecclesiastical History of the English Nation* by the Venerable Bede (New York: Oxford. 1948). This classic eighth-century source history is available in many English translations, including one in the *Everyman's Library.*

*The Pre-Conquest Church in England* by Margaret Deanesly (New York: Oxford. 1961). The newest standard history of the English Church before 1066.

\* *An Introduction to Anglo-Saxon England* by P. H. Blair (New York: Cambridge U. 1959). Excellent chapters on the Church.

*The Saint and the Hunchback* by Donald A. Stouffer (New York: Simon & Schuster. 1946). A novel in which the missionary zeal of the Celtic monks is presented in picturesque detail.

THE CHURCH IN MEDIEVAL ENGLAND

*Medieval England,* ed. by Austin Lane Poole (London: Oxford. New and Revised Edition. 1958. 2 vols.). "Religious Life and Organization in Volume 2, by Dom David Knowles, presents an excellent brief survey.

\* *The English Abbey* by F. H. Crossley (London: Batsford. 1936). One of the best introductions to monastic life. Profusely illustrated.

*The Corner That Held Them* by Sylvia Townsend Warner (New York: Viking. 1948). A novel presenting an accurate and interesting picture of life in a medieval nunnery.

\* *The Canterbury Tales,* Prologue to, by Geoffrey Chaucer. This familiar classic of English literature presents contemporary sketches of figures in the medieval Church.

*Church Life in England in the Thirteenth Century* by J. R. H. Moorman (New York: Macmillan. 1945), and *Pre-Reformation England* by H. Maynard Smith (New York: Macmillan. 1938). Two of the best books available for a careful and detailed study of medieval church life in England. For more advanced reading.

## CHAPTER IV: THE CRISIS OF THE REFORMATION

GENERAL SURVEYS OF THE REFORMATION

\* *The Reformation of the Sixteenth Century* by Roland H. Bainton (Boston: Beacon Press. 1952). One of the best popular books on the Reformation.

*The Crisis of the Reformation* by Norman Sykes (London: Unicorn Press. 1938). An admirable brief discussion.

*Highlights of Church History: The Reformation* by Powel Mills Dawley (Philadelphia: Church Historical Society. 1949). An introductory booklet.

*Renaissance and Reformation Times* by Dorothy Mills (New York: G. P. Putnam's Sons. 1939).

THE REFORMATION IN ENGLAND

*The Reformation in England* by L. Elliott-Binns (London: Duckworth. 1937). Excellent popular study.

*The English Reformation to 1558* by T. M. Parker (New York. Oxford. Home University Library. 1950). A survey of the Reformation from Henry VIII to Elizabeth I.

*Supreme Governor* by J. V. P. Thompson (London: S.P.C.K.). The religious scene under Elizabeth I.

*John Whitgift and the English Reformation* by Powel Mills Dawley (New York: Scribner. 1934). An interpretation of the whole movement.

*Catholic and Reformed* by Florence Higham (London: S.P.C.K. 1962). The English Church in the sixteenth and seventeenth century.

*The English Free Churches* by Horton Davies (New York: Oxford. Home University Library. 1952). English non-conformity in the Reformation era and after.

THE BOOK OF COMMON PRAYER

*The Story of the Prayer Book* by Percy Dearmer (New York: Oxford. 1948). A new edition of the popular *Everyman's History of the Prayer Book*. Well presented and abundantly illustrated.

*A New History of the Book of Common Prayer* by Francis Proctor and W. H. Frere (New York: Macmillan. 1921). The standard text for students and advanced reading.

*The First and Second Prayer Books of Edward VI.* The Prayer Books of 1549 and 1552 are made readily available in *Everyman's Library* (New York: Dutton).

\* *The Worship of the Church* by Massey H. Shepherd, Jr. (New York: Seabury. 1952).

## CHAPTER V: THE CHURCH IN THE MODERN WORLD

GENERAL STUDIES OF THE MODERN CHURCH

*A History of Christianity 1650-1950* by James H. Nichols (New York: Ronald Press. 1956). A standard students' text.

*The Modern Church* by J. W. C. Wand (New York: Crowell). Useful for reference.

\* *The Church and the Age of Reason 1648-1789* by Gerald R. Cragg (Baltimore: Penguin Books. 1960) and *The Church in an Age of Revolution* by Alec R. Vidler (Baltimore: Penguin Books. 1961). Covering the period from the Reformation to the present, these little books are Volumes IV and V in the new excellent Pelican History of the Church.

THE CHURCH OF ENGLAND IN THE MODERN PERIOD

*Anglicanism in History and Today* by J. W. C. Wand (London: Weidenfeld & Nicolson. 1961). An excellent introduction to the history, faith, and life of Anglicanism. Profusely illustrated.

\* *Anglicanism* by Stephen Neill (Baltimore: Penguin Books. 1958). An admirable study of Anglicanism.

*The Evangelical Movement in the Church of England* by L. Elliott-Binns (New York: Doubleday. 1928).

*A Short History of the Oxford Movement* by S. L. Ollard (New York: Morehouse. 1932).

*The Churchman's Heritage* by E. G. Knapp-Fisher (New York: Seabury. 1955). The Anglican heritage. Out of print.

*The Church of England* by Guy Mayfield (New York: Oxford. 1958). The ministry, organization, and work of the Church of England.

THE ANGLICAN COMMUNION

*Frontiers of the Church* by H. G. G. Herklots (London: Ernest Benn. 1961). The story of the missionary expansion of the Church of England and the making of the Anglican Communion.

*One Faith and Fellowship* by John Seville Higgins (New York: Seabury. 1958). The Churches of the Anglican Communion around the world.

* *The Anglican Communion* by Gerald Ellison (New York: Seabury. 1960). A brief introductory treatment.

*Global Odyssey* by Howard A. Johnson (New York: Harper & Rowe. 1963). A report of travels through every part of the Anglican Communion.

THE EPISCOPAL CHURCH

*A History of the American Episcopal Church* by William W. Manross (New York: Morehouse-Barlow. New Edition. 1959). A standard students' text.

*The Episcopal Church in the United States 1789-1931* by James Thayer Addison (New York: Scribner. 1951). An excellent and very readable survey of the Episcopal Church since the American Revolution.

*Our Christian Heritage* by Powel Mills Dawley (New York: Morehouse-Barlow. 1959). An introduction to Church history for Episcopalians, with emphasis on the Episcopal Church.

*Our Expanding Church* by James Thayer Addison (New York: National Council. 1950). The missionary enterprise of the Episcopal Church.

* *The Episcopal Church and Its Work* by Powel Mills Dawley (New York: Seabury. Revised Edition. 1961). The organization, life, and work of the Episcopal Church.

*This Church of Ours,* ed. by Howard A. Johnson (New York: Seabury. 1958). Addresses on the life and thought of the Episcopal Church.

* *The Religion of the Prayer Book* by Walden Pell and Powel Mills Dawley (New York: Morehouse-Barlow. Revised Edition. 1950). An introduction to the teachings of the Prayer Book.

266

ROMAN CATHOLICISM IN THE MODERN WORLD

*The Papacy and Modern Times* by William F. Barry (New York: Oxford Home University Library). A brief sketch on papal history from 1300 to the present day.

* *The Catholic Church in the Modern World* by E. E. Y. Hales (Garden City: Hanover House. 1958). Now an Image Book.

* *The Story of American Catholicism* by Theodore Maynard (New York: Macmillan. 1948).

*Roman Catholicism in England* by E. I. Watkin (New York: Oxford Home University Library. 1957). From the Reformation to the present day.

EASTERN ORTHODOX CHURCHES

*The Eastern Orthodox Church* by R. M. French (New York: Rinehart. 1951). An excellent introduction.

*The Christian Churches of the East* by D. Attwater (Milwaukee: Bruce. 1948).

MODERN PROTESTANT CHRISTIANITY

* *Protestant Christianity* by John Dillenberger and Claude Welch (New York: Scribner. 1954). A standard popular text.

*The Story of Religion in America* by W. W. Sweet (New York: Harper. Edition of 1950). A historical treatment for general reading.

* *Religion in America* by Willard Sperry (New York: Macmillan. 1946). A readable and interesting survey. A Beacon Paper Back.

*The Christian Heritage in America* by George Hedley (New York: Macmillan. 1946). Addresses on various Christian bodies.

*The Presbyterian Churches* by James Moffat (New York: Harper. 1928).

*Presbyterians: Their History and Beliefs* by Walter L. Lingle (Richmond: John Knox Press. Revised Edition. 1960).

*A History of the Baptists* by R. G. Torbet (Philadelphia: Judson Press. 1950).

*A Basic History of Lutheranism in America* by A. R. Wentz (Philadelphia: Muhlenberg Press. 1955).

*Methodism in American History* by W. W. Sweet (Nashville: Abingdon. 1953).

*Methodism* by William B. Brash (New York: Harper. 1928).

*Congregationalism* by Daniel Jenkins (London: Faber & Faber. 1954).

*The Congregational Way of Life* by Arthur A. Rouner (Englewood Cliffs: Prentice-Hall. 1960).

MISSIONARY HISTORY

*An Outline of Missions* by John Aberly (Philadelphia: Muhlenberg Press. 1945).

*Forward through the Ages* by Basil Mathews (New York: Friendship Press. 1951).

THE ECUMENICAL MOVEMENT AND CHURCH UNITY

*The Ecumenical Movement* by Norman Goodall (New York: Oxford. 1961). An explanation of the Movement and the World Council of Churches.

*One Christ, One World, One Church* by Norman Victor Hope (Philadelphia: Church Historical Society. 1953). A brief sketch.

* *Two Centuries of Ecumenism* by Georges H. Tavard (London: Burns & Oates. 1961). An excellent survey by a Roman Catholic scholar.

* *The Anglican Communion in Christendom* by A. E. J. Rawlinson (New York: Seabury. 1960). The Anglican Communion and reunion today.

*The Road to Reunion* by Charles D. Kean (New York: Seabury. 1958). The story of the Episcopal Church and unity conversations and negotiations.

* *Documents in Christian Unity* (New York: Seabury. 1962). Official Episcopal Documents and Resolutions published by the Joint Commission on Approaches to Unity.

*Strangers No Longer* by Peter Day (New York: Morehouse-Barlow. 1962). Admirable popular discussion by an Episcopalian layman.

*On the Road to Christian Unity* by Samuel McCrea Cavert (New York: Harper. 1961). A Protestant approach to the problems of unity.

*Christian Unity* by Charles Boyer (New York: Hawthorn Books. 1962). A Roman Catholic view.

*The Council, Reform and Reunion* by Hans Küng (New York: Sheed & Ward. 1961). An excellent book in which to find examples of the new attitudes of many European Roman Catholic scholars towards Church unity.

# Index